Stop Selling, Start Partnering

Stop Selling, Start Partnering

The New Thinking About
Finding and Keeping
Customers

Larry Wilson
with Hersch Wilson

omneo
An imprint of Oliver Wight Publications, Inc.
85 Allen Martin Drive
Essex Junction, VT 05452

Oliver Wight Publications books may be purchased for educational,
business, or sales promotional use. For information please call or write:
Special Sales Department, Oliver Wight Publications, Inc.,
85 Allen Martin Drive, Essex Junction, VT 05452.
Telephone: (800) 343-0625 or
(802) 878-8161; FAX: (802) 878-3384.

Library of Congress Catalog Card Number: 94-061099

ISBN: 0-939246-74-0

Text design by Joyce C. Weston

Printed on acid-free paper.

Manufactured in the United States of America.

2   4   6   8   10   9   7   5   3

This book is dedicated to my grandchildren, who, when asked the critical question posed by this book, "What is the purpose of business?" responded as follows:

Kif (age thirteen): "To help people communicate and make money. Now get out of my room!"

Corey (age sixteen): "The purpose of business is to make money. It's simple. You can prove me wrong in your book if you want to."

Emily (age six): "The purpose of business is 'cause people have to go to work so they can make money."

Brandon (age six): "For people to work with each other and to cooperate and be good sports and to work and make money for food."

Meghan (age five): "People get more for working at a business and some people think it's fun."

Brynne (age four): "More squeeze cheese, please!"

Casey (age four): "I just don't know what you're talking about!"

Katherine Ann (age two): " 'Cause why!"

Contents

Part IV. How to Create a Partnership 209

Resource Section   255

Foreword

I have spent many years believing that there is nothing more important than selling. Selling is the catalyst, the spark that makes the engine of business run. Successful businesses come in all shapes and sizes, but they all have one thing in common: somebody is doing a good job of selling.

So, when I first heard that Larry Wilson's new book was called *Stop Selling, Start Partnering*, I naturally bristled at the very idea. Stop selling? Why not just close up the doors altogether?

My guess is that if you're reading this, you probably have a connection with selling. You may be a salesperson, or a sales manager, or someone who supports a sales organization. You might even be a buyer. In any of those positions, your first reaction to *Stop Selling* might have been the same as mine. Heresy, right? Goes against everything we believe about business, right?

But consider the source . . .

If you're in selling—or in business, for that matter—you've heard of Larry Wilson. His credits run for pages, but let me just run through the highlights: salesperson for over forty years, founder of Wilson Learning and Pecos River Learning Centers, author, thinker, creator. When it comes to selling, Larry is the authority, as far as I'm concerned. He's "carried a bag" like many of us, calling on clients and looking for better ways to solve a customer's problems. He created Counselor Selling, the groundbreaking training program that transformed a generation of salespeople from the "find 'em, grind 'em" school of selling to the "win-win" approach. And in *Changing the Game: The New Way to Sell*, Larry introduced the key "Strategic Thought Processes" that can help sales professionals find success in a changing environment.

Because of his background, you might think Larry would be the last person to say *Stop Selling*. I know I did. But read further in the title: *Start Partnering*. With this phrase, Larry once again introduces salespeople and sales organizations to a new way to conduct business. And, once again, he makes a lot of sense for anyone whose living depends on successful interactions between a buying and a selling organization. And, to my way of thinking, that's every one of us.

If you don't realize by now that the business world is changing in fundamental ways, you probably won't want to read any further. But if you're like me—and most people involved with selling in any capacity—you are all too familiar with the fact that the old ways of selling, of dealing with customers, of just plain *doing business*, are out the window. Today's business environment calls for new ways to solve customer problems, to build the business, to find success. Salespeople are going to have to think and act differently. And, even then, the salespeople won't be able to do it alone: we'll need *selling organizations*, in which every employee is involved in the sales effort. That's a very different and expanded view of selling. And the reason why *Stop Selling, Start Partnering* is so important.

As usual, Larry's timing is impeccable. When Counselor Selling first hit the training world, selling was basically adversarial in nature. But for many of us out there making the cold calls, getting the rejections, slogging through the mud and mire of 1960s-style selling, we just knew in our guts that there had to be a better way. And along came Larry Wilson with the simple concept that *when I help others get what they want, I get what I want.*

That simple concept is more on the money now—in our era of complex business deals, high leverage financing—than ever before. Taking care of customers is still the golden rule of business.

I predict that the ideas you'll find in *Stop Selling, Start Partnering* will seem just as obvious in twenty-five years. Many sales professionals that I talk to today aren't having the fun they used to. They're finding the world of buying and selling to be tougher, less rewarding, and more stressful than ever before. They have that same nagging feeling that there *must* be a better way

I think Larry Wilson has once again come up with that better way.

You may find the ideas in *Stop Selling, Start Partnering* to be provocative, challenging, and maybe even a little threatening. But I know you'll also find them to be refreshing, insightful, and life-changing. Give them a try—like anything new, they may feel uncomfortable at first, but when you start enjoying success as a result, you'll find them easier and easier to adopt.

As much change as we have experienced, the old saw is still true: "Nothing happens in a business until someone sells something."

I know that the ideas in this book can help you make

something happen. That has been—and is—Larry's genius. He clearly states what we are all experiencing on a daily basis, and prescribes a new philosophy that can take us where we want to go. But there are a lot of business philosophers out there—ivory tower types who presume to know what happens when it's the last day of the quarter and you're 10 percent under quota. Larry has walked in our shoes. He knows the pressure, the defeats, and the triumphs that are part and parcel of selling. And he knows what it's like to be CEO of a multi-million-dollar organization, too. This real-world experience comes through in his down-to-earth, ready-to-use techniques for elevating the way you approach the business of selling.

And, in the end, that's still the heart of any enterprise. *Stop Selling, Start Partnering* will help you take a fresh look at our selling activities, whether you are in the boardroom, face-to-face with customers, or anywhere in between.

—Harvey Mackay
Author of *Swim With the Sharks*

Preface

S *top Selling, Start Partnering* is about thinking differently about customers and, as a result, creating new and more powerful relationships with your best clients. This book is based on the work we do at Pecos River Learning Centers, in which we assist buying and selling organizations come together in partnership.

In our work as a catalyst for partnerships, we use a process called the Strategic Partnering Process, a step-by-step approach that assists buyer and seller to understand the problems and opportunities they face. It also helps them to create the solutions that can result in significant competitive advantage for both organizations. We've organized *Stop Selling, Start Partnering* along the lines of the Strategic Partnering Process.

The first part of the book is the *situation analysis*, addressing such questions as: Where are we now? What is the big picture? What are the critical issues and implications of the current situation? Part II is "Imagining the Future." If we could solve the problems, handle the critical issues, create the perfect solutions, what would it look like? In this section, we describe our vision of the emerging relationships with customers and the selling organization that is being created to keep customers for life. In Part III, we explore the strategic abilities that will help us all be players with the customers and the organizations of the future. In the final part, "How to

Create a Partnership," we'll introduce tactics, a set of specific "tools" to use for creating and sustaining the customer relationships of the future.

Voices

In our work at Pecos River Learning Centers, we don't teach as much as we listen; we don't solve problems for customers as much as we "facilitate" teams of customers in solving problems for themselves. As a result, we constantly hear brilliant ideas, we have the opportunity to talk and argue daily about the future of work, business, and customers with individuals from all over the business landscape, from CEOs of *Fortune* 500 companies to sales managers and salespeople.

With these discussions often lasting long into the night, you can't help but realize that there are a lot of passionate and creative people out there who are making the future happen today. Their beliefs and ideas form a large part of this book, and we wanted you to hear from them in their own voices. So we've included, verbatim, stories, observations, and comments from people like Lou Pritchett, former vice president of sales, Procter & Gamble; Mike Szymanczyk, senior vice president, Philip Morris; Jane Evans, vice president and general manager, US West Communications; Glen Grodem, president and CEO, Smith Furnishings; Jim DeLong, director of sales, Miles, Inc., Agriculture Division; Tamae Moriyasu, salesperson, Hewlett-Packard Company; and dozens of others.

You'll find that these people are not "theorists." They are out there making it happen, testing their creativity and courage against the marketplace and with customers daily. You'll find agreement among them, and some disagreement, too. But they all have valuable contributions to make and they are all committed to the same idea: creating the future of finding and keeping customers.

Acknowledgments

Thanks for the Help!

There is a Yiddish saying, "Life is with people." And so it is with business. Business is with people and writing a book about business has been an ongoing conversation with people from all over the country. These remarkable people would actually politely answer the 8:00 A.M. Saturday phone queries, "What do you think about this idea?" "What would you do if this happened?"

Many of these patient and understanding individuals were customers of Pecos River Learning Centers. They shared with us many of their stories and lessons learned as they create new relationships with their customers. In that light, we'd like to especially thank Lou Pritchett, former vice president of sales, Procter & Gamble, and Mike Szymanczyk, senior vice president, Philip Morris, for their guidance and support.

Many others were critical to the conjuring up and writing of this book. We owe them much: JoAnn Baldinger, who patiently proofed and edited the manuscript, and Lisa Etizone for her graphics and artwork. Carol Fletcher added her insightful and direct feedback. The irrepressible Ronn Lehmann always had ideas, humor, pep talks for the asking. Thank you to Harvey Mackay for his kind words and taking the time from his hectic schedule to put them on paper. We owe many thanks to Tom Haller, who knows as much about selling and partnering today as anyone on the planet. Dan Bodelson knew exactly when it was the right time to have morning creativity meetings at the Santa Fe Ski Basin.

This book would not have been finished without the support of Jill Wenberg and Laurie Wilson. No matter how bleak things looked, how behind schedule we were, they both would fearlessly pop in to the office and ask, "Are you done with it, or what?"

We, of course, owe much to the Pecos River Learning Center staff. They were patient, supportive, curious, and always helpful. To Elizabeth Wilson, the president of Pecos River Learning Centers Inc. and Larry's wife and life partner, we owe a special thanks. This book would never have made it past the idea stage without her support and guidance. She kept us focused on the project, kept our business successful, our employees happy, and our customers satisfied. Thank you, Elizabeth.

Finally, thank you to Jim Childs, our editor at Oliver Wight Publications, for his enthusiasm, support, and direction.

— Larry Wilson and Hersch Wilson

Selling: *The act of influencing, persuading, or inducing someone to purchase a product or service on the basis of superiority, convenience, or price.*

Stop Selling, Start Partnering

Introduction

Finders Keepers, Losers Weepers

We are in the midst of a revolution. It is a revolution that is shaking the foundations of business. But this revolution is not just about the kind of large-scale change that you watch on the evening news. It is more dramatic. This revolution will forever change the basic and the most primal connection of business—the relationship between buyer and seller.

During this revolution, those organizations and individuals who can create new relationships with customers will find themselves with unimagined competitive advantage. Those who don't will lose.

Finders keepers, losers weepers. Those are the rules of this emerging new, challenging, and dramatically different game of business.

Revolution: *A complete change; the overthrow of a social system.*

The very idea of a business and selling revolution is personal to me—as it is to you. I've been a salesperson for forty-five years. It's true that the designation "salesperson" was long ago replaced on my business card with titles like "President" and "CEO." But what I do is sell.

1

My résumé is testament to this fact: I've sold everything from shoes to pension and profit-sharing plans. One fateful year in my early twenties, I moved up from selling vacuum cleaners door-to-door to selling the now forgotten (with good reason!) Crosley car, the only car ever made by a refrigerator company, a subcompact before there were subcompacts, a car so small and cheap that it was an open admission of poverty.

My first true career was as a life insurance salesperson and general agent. Those ten years taught me about selling and customers. That evolved into teaching others to sell, which eventually became Wilson Learning Corporation, the second-largest training company in the country by the early 1980s. In the last fifteen years, I've designed and sold high-end interactive multimedia software and founded and launched our latest venture, Pecos River Learning Centers. But when you boil it all down, I'm still a salesperson. I am still out daily with customers, trying to understand and help them solve their problems.

If you're like me, a salesperson, or a CEO, or anyone who works with customers, this revolution will change everything—our roles and the competencies we need to survive and succeed. This revolution will overthrow the beliefs we hold and the very nature of why we work. It is an exhilarating and scary time to be in business.

And, yet, we all knew that it was coming! Alvin Toffler has written at length about revolutionary change. His first big seller, *Future Shock*, described a future rapid transformation, a future that would completely tax our collective and individual capacities for coping with change. We all read it, agreed with it, and thought, "Yep, out there in the distant future, we'll definitely have to change."

> "No generation has witnessed so many simultaneous changes that are interrelated and of a global nature. . . . On many, many fronts, we're in for a couple of decades of rattling, shaking and reorganization."— Alvin Toffler

Welcome to that future! It's here. Whether we like it or not, Alvin Toffler's gut-wrenching "everything-changing-all-at-once" future is upon us.

My first "stake in the ground" is that the consequences of this future for selling, for salespeople, and for all those who depend on customers for their livelihood are so dramatic and so overwhelming that all our cherished assumptions about selling and customers are up for grabs.

Some Things Never Change

But there is always a paradox. Amidst the revolution, with much changing all around us, one thing hasn't since before the Industrial Revolution. It's the simple, compelling purpose of a business. That purpose was best expressed by the preeminent Harvard Business School professor Theodore Levitt, when he wrote, "The purpose of a business is to find and keep customers and to get existing buyers to continue doing business with you rather than your competitors."

Simple, powerful, and true, and more important now than at any other time in the past forty years.

My second "stake in the ground" is this: to survive and thrive in this business revolution will require everyone who comes to work to rediscover and hold on to that purpose as if it were the most important part of his or her job description—that one objective that makes the difference between keeping a job or being let go.

Why? One of the driving forces of the business revolution is that the world has become astonishingly more competitive. If your company is like most today, you have more competition than ever before—and no doubt some of your competition is coming from overseas, from organizations you had never heard of ten years ago. If you're like many companies today, the products and services you offer, your benefits and prices, are matched point by point by those same competitors. The bottom line is that in the eyes of your customers there is not much difference between what you offer and what your competition offers.

More competitors, tougher customers—difficult business climate, no change in sight, just more "rattling and shaking." The business of finding and keeping customers is now a very high-risk poker game, the consequences of a customer's deciding to go with you or with your competition are more critical to your business now than at any time in recent history.

Faced with this new environment, organizations are waking up and rediscovering that the purpose of *their* business is to find and keep customers. Executives and CEOs are realizing that their job is not to grow shareholder value or to do the fancy financing of mergers and acquisitions—but it is to sell, to find and keep customers. Selling is the highest business purpose of the organization. Selling is no longer a function within the company; it *is* the function of the company.

Dying and Being Born Again

But selling has to be reborn. The old game of selling is dying, victim of the business revolution. The obituary of the old game reads as follows: One salesperson out there bringing in the business, pitching price, features, advantages, and benefits. One salesperson trying to sell as much as he or she can to customers who are trying to avoid being sold, who are trying to get the best price and resist "being taken for a ride."

The old dying game was one salesperson out there battling against the competition for market share and customer mind share. A salesperson who, for all intents and purposes, sold exactly like his or her competition.

The Game of Never Enough

In this game—as any salesperson living it will tell you—there is never enough. There is never enough time, customers, money, or support. There is never enough product, features, price concessions, or territory. And, yet, as those same salespeople will tell you, they are being asked to produce more and more in this same world of never enough.

The causes? Competition, customers, and choices—those are the principal culprits behind the demise of selling. Customers are tougher, they are smarter, they have more choices than ever before. The customers of today can buy better than most salespeople can sell.

Customers have no loyalty, and the world is their shopping mall—there are no national boundaries, only the boundaries of price, convenience, telephone, and faxes.

The point is that you can't win in this game; the traditional beliefs, the sales process, and the training of salespeople are no match for this new customer, for the rising highly competitive and crowded global marketplace. Selling is a dying art.

Fortunately, there is a new game emerging. This future game is more complex but more fulfilling. It is more customer-focused, but it requires the entire selling organization to be involved. Finally, it is a higher-level game, with more risk and more reward.

The New Game: Partnering

Every once in a while you get lucky, and are given an insight into the future. I got my insight into the possible future of selling in the fall of 1991 while working with one of our best customers, Kodak. To help understand how we came to this insight, let me explain a little bit about what we do. Much of the work we do at Pecos River Learning Centers involves helping organizations build teamwork. Our program helps create high levels of trust and collaboration inside organizations.

One day, I was on the phone with Charlie Newton, one of our key contacts at Kodak, and we came up with a radical (at the time) idea. What if we brought a Kodak customer along with the Kodak team responsible for that customer together in a team-building program. What would happen? At first, the reaction was uniformly negative. You can't trust customers. If you let them inside, they will steal you blind. But after that traditional "sales" reaction, we thought about the idea a few more weeks, both intrigued by the possibilities.

Kodak was willing to entertain this idea for a very important reason. This particular division of Kodak produced and sold film to printing companies. Their film had become a commodity, with little differentiation between them and their competitors, like Fuji. The printers down on the presses didn't care what film they used. The only differences they, the experts, saw between vendors were the color of the boxes. So Kodak's motivation was to differentiate themselves with their key customers. The idea was simple. Kodak was a one-hundred-year-old company with all kinds of profit-improvement processes that they used internally. Couldn't their customers, who were smaller, with fewer resources, benefit from the same ideas? It seemed like a good plan. But first they had to get customers to participate with them at a different level, to move away from the typical adversarial seller-buyer relationship.

Kodak found a customer who was interested, a company that had been buying from Kodak for ten years. Yet, although Kodak had been calling on them regularly, they were buying only $200,000 of product from Kodak out of $1.5 million annually allocated for film.

Kodak convinced this customer to send representatives to spend a week with them in New Mexico to discuss new ways of working together. This was different from playing golf together; this was different from the traditional "We'll take you to a ball game." The weeklong meeting was an investment in time and money for both companies to reinvent a relationship. And it wasn't just the Kodak sales team and the buyers from the printing company, it was a vertical slice from both organizations. Everyone who had a stake in the relationship came to the session. The president of the printing company was there, as were printers from the shop floor.

The first evening, they explored the possibilities of a new relationship. There was lots of skepticism in the room and some tension. There was a lot of history, not all of it good, between the two organizations. The printing company was quite happy with their dominant supplier. The Kodak people were a little defensive about being blamed for problems that they didn't believe were caused by them.

Yet, over the next few days, they got to know each other, and they began—for the first time—to understand each other's problems and the opportunities that existed. The conversation shifted; they stopped talking about product, and they stopped "naming and blaming."

The group turned to discussing how to help the customer—the printing company in an extremely competitive and costly business. The feeling in the room at that time was electric. Thirty people, from all over the two organizations, who had traditionally kept each other at arm's length, were now going full tilt in long sessions, attempting to help the printing company do three things: make money, save money, and add value to their customer. What I saw, from the back of the room, was this: it was not a buyer and seller "negotiating" price, not a seller trying to move as much product as possible on to a buyer and the buyer resisting.

Instead, it was one team of people identifying and eliminating all the barriers that existed between the two companies, the barriers that hindered their ability to work together and hindered both of them from being as profitable as they could be. For me, this was a glimpse of what the future held for finding and keeping customers in a world of intense competition. This was the new game.

One of the most telling moments of the week we spent together was when the group from the printing company asked for some time to meet by themselves. They met to discuss how to tell their dominant vendors that they were moving all the business to Kodak. They weren't discussing "if"—they were discussing how to do it.

It was a transformative meeting for them; it changed how

they saw each other and how they worked together. For me, it was watching the birth of a brand-new kind of relationship. The folks from Kodak and from their customer organization used the word "partnership" to express what they felt was the difference between the old way and the new.

Creating and sustaining partnerships with customers is the new way. These relationships are part of the solution to the intensely competitive, revolutionary times we live in. Partnering will replace selling in our lexicon of best practices.

But what does this mean for us as salespeople, as CEOs— or as anyone who works with customers? Fundamentally, it means all of our roles will change. Playing this new game is akin to moving from baseball, which is tradition-bound, where everyone knows the rules and the roles, to something brand-new, like soccer.

At first, soccer looks like chaos. The players are running around a field madly kicking a ball, the uniforms are wildly colorful and different, and it is hard to tell the players apart. The pace of the game changes in a matter of seconds. The clock is always running; there are no time outs and no substitutions allowed. Then, all at once, structure emerges, a play comes together, a team scores, and then, to the untrained eye, it goes back to players running around the field aimlessly. But after watching for a while, the rules, the roles, and the structure emerge.

Here is our opportunity as salespeople, CEOs, and the "customer workers" of today. We are standing at the edge of this field, watching this brand-new game begin. If we want to thrive in this new world, if we want to survive the business revolution, then we will have to learn this game—we will have to learn the reasons, the rules, and the roles. It promises to be faster, more complex, with new and different players, than ever before. The risks are greater, and so are the rewards. It will not be for everyone, but for those companies and for those salespeople who choose to play, it promises to be exciting and profitable—and in business it doesn't get better than that.

For those who choose not to learn and play in this new game, who choose to remain as players in the old game of selling, the risk is just as great. The business revolution is sweeping away many of our traditional ways of working, of interacting with customers. If we don't change, if we don't embrace the future, we will be left behind.

The greatest risk of all is that we will end up being the best players in a game no longer being played. The consequences of not changing, of not keeping ahead of the game, are the grist of the daily business news. For example, in the spring of 1994, IBM, in what the *Wall Street Journal* called a stunning change, fired forty advertising firms and consolidated all its advertising work with one vendor. A $500 million switch. Obviously, much went on behind the scenes to make that deal happen, but at some level, a sales team (whether they were salespeople, executives, or the CEO of the winning advertising firm) sold IBM on the idea that they could make a significant difference for IBM. The sales team convinced IBM that they could help them make money, save money, or add value to their customers by an order or magnitude greater than IBM was doing previously.

These types of relationships are the future. Partnerships, single sourcing, long-term relationships are what companies—both buyers and sellers—will be looking for. And they will be looking to their salespeople, the best and the brightest, to create them. The business landscape is changing radically, the players, the relationships are being altered daily. New alignments are arising, old relationships are being dissolved. Partnerships, consolidations on one hand; other companies and salespeople being cast out into the outer darkness on the other.

Finders keepers, losers weepers: *It will be dramatic, the deals and partnerships will be significant. The winners will thrive, the losers will struggle. Those are the consequences of the new game.*

The Forecast Is for Change

At one level, *Stop Selling, Start Partnering* is a business book, pure and simple. Yet, there is also a more personal element at work here. I can best describe this personal aspect by telling a story about a "wake-up call" I experienced a few years ago.

In 1982, I sold Wilson Learning Corporation and moved to my current home in Santa Fe, New Mexico. For reasons I still don't quite understand, I decided to build a conference center on a two-thousand-acre ranch in the mountains of northern New Mexico, outside the sleepy village of South San Ysidro, forty miles from Santa Fe and two hours from the nearest airport. It was my version of "If I build it, they will come." I believed that organizations would bring their people to this quiet, breathtakingly beautiful place to do whatever companies do when they have conferences. (Hey, it was the eighties!)

Well, it remained a sleepy little village and a sleepy little conference center—because no one came. I was fifty-four years old, trying to launch a brand-new business and, to put it politely, it was failing. Having a failing business and a lot of debt can be an amazingly focusing experience. Although that wasn't the first time I had skirted the edge, I realized that I could go bankrupt. It was a scary time in my life and I worried myself to sleep many nights, churning through the possibilities and the solutions.

But, as a lot of organizations are discovering today, the crisis of potential failure brings you right back to that fundamental purpose: finding and keeping customers. For us, as the money hemorrhaged, as the bank and my family became increasingly nervous, we weren't concerned about *keeping* customers so much as scrambling to *find* them—find one! We knew we had to develop reasons for companies to come to the newly named Pecos River Learning Centers.

We discovered that many companies were looking for ways to empower their people to handle change and cope successfully with the transforming world economy. Working with potential customers, we designed and began offering programs that would fill those needs. In line with the radical changes most companies were facing, our programs were fairly radical for those times, designed to impact individual and organizational resistance to and fear of change.

The programs incorporated an outdoor day, with "ropes course" activities. During a full day outside, people faced a number of challenges both individually and as a team, including rock climbing, rappelling, and zipping down a cable off a cliff. The ropes course is intense, a powerful experience that challenges all our preconceived notions about ourselves and our limitations. Combining the outdoor day with some classroom experiences, we created our first program, which we called "Changing the Game." Its purpose was to help the top team of an organization create the passion and commitment required to lead that organization into the future. Individuals and companies began to trickle down to the Pecos River Ranch as word spread that we were on to something that could help companies prepare for the future.

So there I was, in debt up to and beyond my eyeballs, the clock ticking down, with a fledgling product just being launched. Understandably, my tension level was extremely high. I wanted everything to be perfect and was micromanaging every detail, from how the rooms looked to what the instructors said and did. I was also driving everyone who worked with me nuts.

According to a number of my colleagues, I was irrational about it. I remember watching a team out on the ropes course one day. Above them, a wild western New Mexico thunderstorm began to build. Thunder rumbled very close by. As the weather closed in, the rain began to fall, lightning crashed on the ridges surrounding us, and I saw my whole business washing away down the arroyos.

Thunderstorms, blizzards, the occasional monsoonlike downpours—these could ruin me because clients wouldn't finish the outdoor day, they would be unhappy, they would say bad things about us, customers would stop coming, and I would go broke and die penniless—or so went my stream of consciousness. Did I mention I was a bit irrational about this?

So I wanted to control the weather. Hey, I was the CEO, the owner of this ranch, and I deserved to be in control! Right? But there was a problem. The weather in mountainous northern New Mexico is completely unpredictable. The standing joke is "If you don't like the weather, wait twenty minutes and it will change." Often we end up getting the opposite of what we intend, and for a while there the weather controlled me. I was happy when the weather cooperated, angry when it rained, and furious when it snowed on a ropes course day. As if the weather cared.

I was spending a lot of energy railing against the weather, as if that would make a difference. At some point, I finally realized that the weather is the weather is the weather. It comes and goes, it's awful or glorious, and it's totally out of my control. Carrying the thought a step further, I came to a blinding flash of the obvious: there really is no such thing as bad weather—it's just weather. The problem is that we are often unprepared for what it might bring.

When you know the weather might bring anything from drought to monsoon, you prepare for it. You plan for all possibilities. You bring what you might need, so that when it rains, you can stay dry. You don't show up in shorts and a T-shirt and then get mad when it snows.

I had been totally unprepared for building a conference center in the middle of New Mexico. I had no idea what I was getting into, no notion of the factors that could lead to failure or to success. We ended up depending on miracles: the customers who showed up and loved us, the right people who turned up to work with us. We have been blessed with an abundance of those kinds of miracles.

But depending on miracles is a tough way to learn to run a new business. It's also a tough way to prepare for success in the unpredictable weather that we all now face.

Today, as we look toward a new century, the future is a lot like the weather in New Mexico: completely unpredictable. We have no idea what it will look like, except it will *not* be like the past. The future is going to be strange and uncomfortable—and full of potential for those individuals and companies that are prepared.

How do you prepare for the unpredictable?

> "The future will require individuals to have everything from snorkels to life preservers to wings. You will need to be prepared for anything."
> — Jane Evans, Vice President and General Manager, Small Business Group, US West Communications

First, and most important, prepare yourself for change. Prepare to "let go" of many of the beliefs, behaviors, and ways of working that have been with us for decades, because they may not work in the future. Adopt the posture of the learner; open yourself up to new possibilities, new ways of seeing the world, your customers, and yourself. Develop the inner strength necessary to cope with great change, to cope with high levels of ambiguity and risk. Instead of waiting for miracles, or denying that change is happening, prepare for it, just as you prepare for bad weather.

Get ready for an adventure, because that is what's in store for all of us.

> "We cannot put off living until we are ready. The most salient characteristic of life is its coerciveness; it is always urgent, here and now without any possible postponement. Life is fired at us point blank." — José Ortega y Gasset

Part One

~~~~~~~~~~

Permanent White Water

Imagine this. Your travel agency calls and tells you about an exciting vacation package. The agent admits that it is a little different from other trips they've offered. To start with, she can't tell you where you are going. Nor can she be certain that you will arrive at your destination. Finally, she tells you that the trip starts tomorrow and you need to buy your ticket immediately.

Most of us would reject that offer out of hand, without even thinking about it. But the truth is that we are all on that journey. The journey is the future. We are embarking into the future and we don't know where we are going and we are not sure we're going to get there. The only difference between the imaginary trip and reality is that in reality we have no choice. We're taking that trip. We are bound for an uncertain future—otherwise known as an "adventure."

One of the most vivid descriptions of this adventure was coined by Georgetown Business School professor Peter Vaill. He labeled this journey as a voyage through "permanent white water," conjuring up images of constant, unpredictable change. We're in the middle of massive turbulence, never knowing from which direction the next fabulous opportunity

> "Even the wisest of them were at a hopeless disadvantage, for their only guide to sorting it out--the only guide anyone ever has—was the past, and precedents are worse than useless when facing something entirely new."
> — William Manchester, *A World Lit Only by Fire,* about the fifteenth century on the verge of the Renaissance

or crippling body blow will come. There is no calm water, no resting place in sight. If you look for precedents, there aren't many; the future can no longer be predicted by remembering the familiar and comfortable signposts of the past.

In the next three chapters, we are going to analyze the current situation, look at the causes and consequences of this revolution. We want to look beneath the white water and get at what is really going on, what themes are emerging and impacting your business and your customer's business. Since we are all in this boat together, from the boardroom to the factory floor, we've divided these chapters into three perspectives. The first perspective is that of senior management. From their point of view, their marketplace has become global, intensely competitive, with unprecedented pressures on the bottom line. The perspective of sales management is framed by the question, in these expensive and highly competitive times, "Do we really need a sales force?" If so, how small can it be and what should it be doing? Finally, we'll look at this new world from the perspective of salespeople and customers. Clearly, the power once held by the manufacturer and the salesperson has been wrenched away by the customer, and that has completely changed the meaning of the word "selling."

Let's begin by looking at change through the glasses of senior management—the individuals responsible for guiding the ship.

Chapter One

〰〰〰〰

"We're Not Going to Just Blow Away"

Fear, exhilaration, and surging adrenaline. Opportunities abound, if only they can be seen, understood, and exploited quickly. The ups and downs are steep and unrelenting, there are shoals and rocks everywhere, the current is powerful, and companies are being swept away. Senior management's perspective is that of the helmsman, looking far downriver and seeing nothing but unrelenting white water.

The predictable, tranquil waters of the past thirty or so years are gone and, as we all have seen, today even the largest and most powerful of ships can run aground.

A recent illustration is Wang Laboratories. Back in the heyday of word processing, Wang was a big customer of my former company, Wilson Learning Corporation, and we were a customer of theirs. For all intents and purposes, Wang invented word processing. They had the best software and the best systems. The end users—writers, secretaries, attorneys, and just about anyone who ever toiled with a typewriter—loved Wang. The story is told that Dr. Wang, the founder, walked through the United Nations offices one day and all the secretaries and assistants gave him a standing ovation because they loved their "Wangs" so much. That is customer loyalty to die for.

After selling Wilson Learning in the mid-1980s, I stopped keeping track of Wang. So, in 1992, I was shocked to read in the *Wall Street Journal* that Wang had declared Chapter 11. What was poignant and telling about the times we live in was one of the quotes they used in the article. In 1989, Frederick Wang, the son of the founder, said, "We're a three-billion-dollar company. We're not going to just blow away."

In high-tech industries, the current is particularly swift and capricious. Yet, in retrospect, there are no surprises here. Anyone who dealt with Wang could have predicted as early as the mid-eighties that trouble was brewing, even when Wang was the darling of Wall Street. Which goes to show that Wall Street knows little about what truly makes a business successful. Wang was never known for being customer-focused or service-oriented. Instead, it was "product-driven." To Wang, products were the key to success, and they behaved as if they were the *only* key. They were slow to adapt to the dramatically changing world of information management, to the fact that all those other computer suppliers were catching up—and fast.

Think of this: Wang went from a start-up company to a multi-billion-dollar international corporation ranked 146 on the *Fortune* 500 list, and then to Chapter 11 bankruptcy, all within forty years. Wang was sailing full speed ahead when it hit permanent white water.

This is the reality of the nineties. Size doesn't provide immunity; size can hinder change and adaptation. Innovation doesn't provide automatic immunity, either. No one is immune anymore. There is very little margin for error, very little room to maneuver, and misjudgments can cause dramatic, dire, and breathtakingly swift consequences. Management must make lightning-quick decisions, and they have to be right. The river is relentless and stops for no one.

Falling Dominoes

Permanent white water is a result of societal and technological changes. But a major cause of the business white water from the perspective of senior management lies deep in the fundamentals of a business.

The formula is simple. Most CEOs could chart the causes on a napkin. Rapidly expanding global competition has helped create tough, demanding, and fickle customers who, because they have lots of choices, have punished their suppliers over prices, resulting in plummeting margins and profits.

Without profits, most companies have little room to maneuver. Without profits, companies die. And all this is happening at unprecedented speed. Calling the problem "simple" doesn't mean it's easy to solve. "Simple" doesn't even mean that every company, awash in the current, is aware of what is happening or is taking steps to prepare for a future of even more white water.

And, so, the dominoes begin to fall . . .

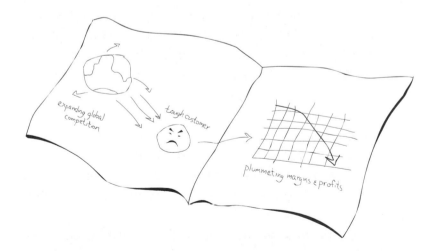

Domino No. 1: Global Competition

"The market and the world have changed. We no longer live in a solo market. Twenty years ago, you didn't care what the exchange rate was. Now you have to track the yen and the pound because they can affect your income. The world has shrunk dramatically."
— George Brown, Chairman of the Board, Jardine Insurance Brokers, Inc.

The first domino: intense and growing competition from around the globe. Name any industry; chances are that today there is either an increase in competitors entering the market or a declining customer base. Or, in some cases, both! The net result is the same: competition in price, value, quality, and speed, all on a scale unparalleled in American industrial history.

But don't make the mistake of thinking that the world is as competitive as it can get—this is only the beginning. Let's look ahead to the next century by looking back fifty years. In 1945, the United States was the only industrialized nation untouched by the devastation of two world wars. American business had no competition. The world was borrowing money from us to buy our products, and we could set prices and standards based solely on what our markets could bear. The marketplace had three colors: red, white, and blue.

As our standard of living increased, our prices went up. As demand went up, quality became less of an issue to the customer. Consumers threw away or traded in items that they didn't like.

A cyclical but always growing economy was a powerful

and pervasive drug. It anesthetized us to what was happening in the rest of the world. Business was so good that many large organizations stopped thinking about products, innovation, service, and customers and thought only about making money. Increased costs were simply passed on to the consumer. Everybody did it and it wasn't a problem, because, for the most part, wages were rising at approximately the same rate. The money rolled in and stock prices rose—the American business dream come true. It was our century, so the thinking went.

"Over there," meanwhile, the rest of the world was shaking off the effects of thirty years of world wars, of hyperinflation, depressions, and rebuilding their economies (with our help, of course).

By the 1970s, some of our former students had begun flexing their industrial strength, and were turning into full-fledged world competitors. The first shock to our system was delivered by the Japanese. We lost entire industries, like consumer electronics, to a hungrier, more quality- and consumer-focused competitor.

But the Japanese were only the beginning. Germany wasn't far behind. And now we are starting to hear from countries whom we never in our wildest dreams imagined as competitors, countries we pejoratively labeled "Third World" countries (because they would never "measure up") including Mexico, India, and the People's Republic of China. The young tigers of South Korea, Malaysia, Vietnam, Singapore, and other Asian nations are coming up fast.

The list of emerging competitors gets longer and stronger every day. Just look around the world. The irony is that we have won the political battle of capitalism over communism, convincing country after country that the road to prosperity is through some sort of free market economy. The problem is that they are taking it seriously! And when it comes to a competitive environment, some economists warn that if Russia and the other countries of the former USSR, with their vast natural resources and population of 300 million, ever get their act together, and the European Union continues to move forward as planned, the world—and your market-place—will resemble a crowded supermarket shelf where there are seemingly hundreds of choices of products that all look and are priced the same.

Lou Pritchett, the former vice president of sales for Procter & Gamble, knows the challenge of international competition firsthand. Lou oversaw a vast sales effort that encompassed virtually every part of the globe. As a result, he is an expert on what all this competition might mean for us. "We have yet to see the full impact of the open, global marketplace," Lou says. "I'm convinced, for instance, that by the year 2000, all raw materials and technology will be available everywhere in the world. The only differences between countries and markets will be the levels of skill, education, and empowerment among the workforce."

What does this mean for you? What will your business be like when all those countries, and all those companies, are powerful industrial forces competing for your market share? They will be hungry for what we have. They will work long hours and, in the beginning, they will work for less. They will exploit competitive weaknesses just as the Japanese ex-ploited the quality gap.

"Even if you're on the right track, if you stand still you'll get run over." — Will Rogers

Most senior managers understand all too well that if their companies are not awake to the global challenge, competitors will surround them and eat them alive. If they are asleep, there will be price competition—companies that can imitate them, and do it cheaper. If they are asleep, there will be companies that add more value. There will be companies that will innovate around them. Finally, if they stand still, there will be competitors who will lock them out of new customers through single-source relationships. Those competitors might be next door, or they might be halfway around the world. Armed with a fax machine and a telephone, your global competitor will be talking and proposing to your customer whose workplace is only two blocks from you!

Imagine your business in ten years. Imagine that there are no regulatory boundaries and that you have ten new competitors from overseas.

✔ *How would your business change?*

✔ *How would you keep the customers you currently have?*

✔ *How would you find new worldwide customers? How would you exploit new markets?*

✔ *How will your company learn to thrive in a world market?*

Domino No. 2: The Customer Revolution

Intense, global competition of this unprecedented nature pushes over the next domino: the loyal, predictable customer. The sleeping giant, the customer, is waking up and beginning to flex serious muscle. And this is not a happy giant.

✔ *What happens when competition increases dramatically? Customer loyalty and customer predictability nose-dive.*

Historically, large organizations have been "factory out," product-driven, and a touch arrogant about it. A product-driven strategy has at its core the belief that, if we make it, somebody out there will buy it. Again, this was a hugely successful strategy in the quarter-century following World War II, and it shaped the beliefs and behaviors of generations of executives. The customer was a mass market: faceless, nameless, all alike and impersonal. We believed that the mass market would continue to increase in numbers and demand for what we sold. Customers were predictable, markets were predictable, and consumers were easily influenced, i.e., manipulated.

Toss another cherished belief into the Dumpster.

Give customers more options and they jump ship—fast. Why? The undiscussable truth is that customers have not been treated as important in the overall scheme of things. But customers couldn't do much about it in the past. Today, with more choices, they can do a lot! If customers don't quite like the color and the options you provide, well, they can walk across the mall—or, figuratively, across the Pacific and find exactly what they want. If customers don't feel that they are being treated as they deserve to be treated, ditto. Customers are demanding, fussy, and volatile, and their expectations are rising continually.

This is the era of mass customization. Customers want solutions tailored explicitly to their situations. The question for many businesses now is not how large is the market for a product or service, but how can we adapt and customize

"The large market segments of the past are gone forever. The winners in today's marketplace are ones who understand micro-marketing. Today, people act in more of a tribal mode according to everything from demographics to religious beliefs to various income—These are small, shifting, and situational alliances. The idea of breaking the market down into nice little boxes—it's not going to work anymore." — Phil Styrlund, US West

products and services for the smallest markets, or that one industrial customer, and still make money?

In that light, customers rarely are interested in *your* organization's definitions of service and quality; they have their own and they are different for every customer. This customer expects Just-in-Time delivery, the next requires a defect rate lower than you've ever produced. The next requires unique packaging that fits into their work-flow process, but has little to do with how packaging has always been done In the industry.

These same customers are no longer bound by political or geographic boundaries; they can go wherever they want in order to get the quality and prices they want. Information technology makes it possible for consumers to shop around the world.

How long before we will be able to dial 1-800-Japan or 1-800-France for consumer goods and charge them on Visa or American Express?

How long before we can order a customized Honda or Saturn from a video display and have the car delivered to our home the next week?

Technology like that will outstrip the regulators, overwhelm trade barriers, and move faster than many companies will be able to tolerate. Unless there is a world war, or a worldwide depression (both unlikely), technology, customers, and their megadollars will drive the world toward highly competitive, completely open markets no matter what the politicians want, no matter the restrictive trade policies.

Who is going to drive the new world economy? Not governments, not regulations, but powerful, sophisticated consumers. We will play their game, or we won't play!

✔ *How well do you know your customers?*

✔ *What do your customers require?*

✔ *What will they require next year? In five years?*

✔ *What are your customers imagining their futures will look like?*

✔ *What are your customers' customers imagining their futures will look like?*

Domino No. 3: Everything Is a Commodity

Keeping this increasingly demanding and sophisticated customer is clearly a imperative, right? But how? The old way was to have the best products, the best prices. That is still important; but in a much more competitive world, the benchmarks for products and price are rapidly being met by many of your competitors. It's like the airlines. One cuts prices by 40 percent; that same day, boom!—they all do it! So much for price advantage. Pick any industry, and you will find products, services, and prices all beginning to look alike, to blur together. To the customer, even salespeople all tend to look alike. They ask the same questions, wear the same suits, write the same proposals, make the same promises. From the customer's point of view, there is not a lot of differentiation out there.

Welcome to the next falling domino: the rule of commodities. Intense competition often boils down to the fact that, *from the vantage point of the customer*, the only difference between your product and the products of your twenty competitors is the different-colored boxes they come in.

✔ *The product or service you spend all that money on manufacturing, distributing, and selling is seen by customers as a commodity, undifferentiated except by minute variations in price or convenience.*

Another sign of our times is that with so little differentiation, companies are having to "buy" their business. For example, there is so little difference (from the customer's point of view) between long-distance phone carriers—AT&T and MCI—that both carriers will pay a prospect to switch to their service.

We are all moving toward that kind of competitive environment. No matter how innovative and differentiated we are now, all signs point toward becoming commodities. Most products and services begin life competitively. But exposed to the market, they eventually become commodities. This has always been so. The difference today, because of intense competition, open markets, and rapid communication, is that products move down the slippery slope to become commodities almost overnight.

Which brings us to Federal Express, a prime example of

how the commodity rule stalks businesses today. Federal Express started with an innovative idea. Overnight package delivery was so new when Fed Ex started that they often would have more airplanes on the ramp than packages. But then the idea "took off," and in the seventies, "Fed Ex" became synonymous with overnight delivery and launched a billion-dollar-plus industry. Yet, in less than twenty years, Fed Ex has gone from innovation to commodity.

Even ten years ago, in our mailroom, "sending it overnight" meant, by definition, Federal Express. Today, sending it overnight can mean Federal Express, UPS, Airborne, or the United States Postal Service. The decision is made by our shipping manager, who has no emotional attachment to Federal Express and makes decisions on a price and convenience basis.

What is happening to Fed Ex is occurring in every industry. The cycle time from competitive innovation to commodity is becoming frighteningly brief. Today, the cycle is even faster, especially in high technology.

> "The time frame for products has become so compressed that we no longer have the luxury of market testing. There is always a competitor right on your tail. Now it is how fast can you be, how flexible can you be, how customized can you be?"
> — Jane Evans, Vice President and General Manager, US West Communications

Think of a product in three broad categories, each with specific characteristics. The most important principle is that products are seen from the customer's point of view. Over time, products and services evolve from innovative to commodity.

INNOVATIVE → COMPETITIVE → COMMODITY

■ The Innovative Product
No competition.
Unique business niche.
Ability to set initial pricing strategies.
Ability to lock in customer relationships.

■ The Competitive Product
Product differentiation from customer's point of view.
Unique specifications.
Ability to charge higher price.
More difficult for customer to switch to a different
    vendor.

■ The Commodity Product
Little or no product differentiation from customer's
    point of view.
Commonly shared specifications.
Downward price pressure, typically a low-margin sale.
Buyers make their buying decisions on a sale-by-sale
    basis.
The buyer's focus is purchasing a prespecified
    product at the lowest possible price.
Buyers are not locked into any one vendor and can
    easily switch vendors at any time with minimum
    inconvenience.

✔ *Are your products Innovative or Commodities?*

✔ *Where will they be in a year? In two years?*

✔ *Who is the innovative leader in your industry?*

✔ *Who is the value-added leader?*

✔ *Who is the low cost provider?*

✔ *How are you closing the gap on all of the above?*

Accelerating the commoditization of most industries are rapidly changing technologies, fast and open access to information, world competition, and smart, smart customers.

> "We have to produce more pieces to meet more specific customer needs. My people want raises every year. My taxes are going up. My distribution costs are going up. It's so damned competitive now. Every time I turn around, someone is giving 5 percent away to buy the business. You can't make the margins you want, you don't have a lot of room to move around, and you are left with your prime expenses—60 percent of which are people. Guess what has to go! That's the senior management dilemma."
> — Jim DeLong, Director of Sales, Miles, Inc., Agriculture Division

The Last Domino You Heard Crash Was Profits

The domino effect continues. Unprecedented global competition has helped create tough world-class customers who see little difference between our products or services. As a result, given few alternatives, they attack price. The result is the fall of a large domino: tremendous pressure on margins and profitability. Profits, the lifeblood of companies, are under attack as never before in recent history.

When profits nose-dive, they take a lot with them, including the ability to invest in research, development of new products, and people. That sets in motion a vicious circle. Without leading-edge products, it becomes even more difficult to retain high margins and profitability, leading to cutting of budgets and jobs, which inhibits the creation of new products . . . and the cycle of cost and capability cutting continues.

Among the social casualties of this last domino are the expectations of employees. Walk into any struggling company, large or small, experiencing the cycles of layoffs, restructurings, redeployments, downsizings, and the unspoken but palpable question is "Am I next?" The social contract between employer and employee has been torn apart by permanent white water and the business revolution. There is no more employment for life. There are no more tenured, secure jobs. Even in those last bastions of secure employment, hospitals and government, employment is at risk.

In the 1980s, while the undercurrents were building for this momentous change, things seemed normal on the surface. Businesses were growing, wealth was being created, and many structural problems could be ignored. Employee expectations were rising. When the dominoes began to fall, companies and individuals were totally unprepared for the depth and breadth of the restructuring that is occurring in our economy. Many an expectation has been lowered, if not permanently smashed.

"In the 1990s, the economy is flat, price competition has heated up, and margins have come down. It's sad, because in the eighties, we had so much explosive growth that allowed a lot of people—middle management, in particular—to become pretty affluent. Now, all of a sudden, all that has come to a screeching halt. It has caused a lot of pain and changed a lot of lives."
— Mike Szymanczyk, Senior Vice President, Sales, Philip Morris

What Keeps You Up at Night?

These dominoes are falling across all industries: wrenching change, competition coming out of the woodwork, and exploding costs. The double-edged sword of technology replacing people constantly dangles in front of you. All the stakeholders in the business—customers, shareholders, employees, communities—are angry, upset over change, and demanding answers. And there are not a lot of easy or immediate answers. For the first time in the experience of many individuals and many companies, the people at the top no longer have the answers. In some cases, they don't have a clue as to what is going on or what to do about it.

For those individuals who are in the second or third decade of managing large organizations, that once secure and somewhat privileged world is being turned upside down by factors that were not even discussed or thought of ten years ago. The past is no longer a guide, the future looks, at best, chaotic.

The Death of the Corporate Gods

In the early 1970s, *Time* magazine ran a controversial and thought-provoking cover story that asked, "Is God dead?" A similar, though less theological, question is now being posed in the halls of many companies: "Where are the folks who used to have all the answers?"

Mike Szymanczyk, senior vice president of sales at Philip Morris, has been involved in more than a few organizational restructurings as he tried to keep ahead of the fast-moving consumer package-goods business. In the process, he has learned a lot about what happens when an organization hits this kind of change. He says: "In many large, traditional organizations, there is an attitude that there are 'corporate gods' at the top with all the answers. I remember thinking, as a young manager at Procter & Gamble, 'Boy, those guys at the top are really smart and they've got everything figured out.' The belief becomes that as long as you make sacrifices to the corporation and bend to its whims, it will take care of you. The 'corporate gods' start believing it as well. It is fun being served, it's very ego-rewarding to have people defer to you and reinforce your ideas, even the bad ones. Now the corporate gods are being exposed as not having all the answers and not being able to solve all the problems. It's like the Wizard of Oz—senior management behind the curtain, pulling all the levers, pushing the buttons, often without knowing what's really going on."

Crisis

Mix this all together, add new technologies, add political and social upheaval, and the result is massive, dislocating, structural change. This is the big picture. By almost every definition, we are at a turning point, moving toward a decisive change in how we do business and how we work together. In a crisis, there is always pain, especially for the companies and individuals who are caught by surprise, who haven't prepared for the weather.

This message is difficult for people to hear. It is equally difficult to write about, because no one likes to see people hurt. No one likes to see individuals who have put in twenty or thirty years with the same company out of a job, no matter the reasons. No one likes to hear that there aren't any answers, or at least there aren't any easy ones.

Finally, no one (especially me!) likes to be the prophet of hard times. But this is reality: for the next ten or twenty years, permanent white water, crisis and opportunity, will be "condition normal." We are riding a raft down a wild river, and around every bend, when we think it must surely calm down, there is only wilder water. Our only choice is to learn to thrive in the rapids.

> Life is a series of collisions with the future.
> — José Ortega y Gasset

Chapter Two

〰〰〰〰〰〰

The Death of a Sales Force

Selling will not escape the turmoil of white water. Selling has been a career for generations of individuals, yet it is about to endure massive rattling and shaking.

I grew up in a family supported by selling, by a father who was on the road. Some of my most vivid memories are going with my father to sales conventions. We would always drive in my father's Cadillac—he bought a new one every three years to impress his customers (and us). A suit, a fedora, and his cigar were mandatory on those trips. It was the era of big business and my father was a company man. The military model of organizing the company was the way it was in those days: the company told you when to get married, where to live, and what your job was. Part of the routine was the national sales convention every year. Those conventions were in huge auditoriums and were filled with, at the time, mostly salesmen and just a few women. There were awards banquets, golf tournaments, and lots of parties. Energy and enthusiasm were the prime ingredients at most of those meetings, and most of the faithful went home ready to knock 'em dead and destroy the competition for another year.

Later on, as a sales trainer and motivational speaker, I spent at least twenty years speaking to those same audiences. The styles changed, the suits changed, left, and came back into style, but there were always convention halls packed with salespeople.

That was the way it was. Companies had a *sales force* out there knocking on doors, handling the territories, making the business happen. Volume was the key and salespeople spent day in and day out "drumming up business." Management went to sleep at night knowing that they had legions of folks out knocking on customer doors, sometimes all over the world.

Today, sales management loses sleep wondering if traditional selling—and that sales force—is part of the solution or part of the problem.

> "I think the traditional sales organization is a dinosaur, a remnant of a past success."
> — Rick Canada, Director, Change Management
>   Services, Motorola

If you are out there knocking on doors, that is a scary pronouncement. I'm writing this on an airplane on my way to a sales call on a potential new customer. I look around and see lots of salespeople earning a living as they have done for decades: on the road, seeing customers face-to-face, battling the home office over expenses, commissions, and sales forecasts. Meanwhile, the world is about to change as much and as dramatically for salespeople as it has for middle management, that formerly vast group of workers who are disappearing from the workforce.

Selling has become too expensive, too risky, and, in many cases, unnecessary. Selling is increasingly becoming a game that customers no longer want to play—or pay for, either directly or indirectly.

The domino effect—the effect of increased competition, demanding customers, new technologies, and the commoditization of most products and services—is transforming the game of direct selling.

Transaction Reaction

Step back and look at the relationship between buyer and seller and how it has changed as the world has become more competitive. With more options that look alike and are sold alike, buyers make decisions to go with one product or another on the basis of what difference is left: price and convenience. Customers buy the best price and the most convenient arrangement from the options presented. Note that I didn't say they were *sold* the best price or most convenient arrangement. In this kind of relationship, buyers are capable of making their own decisions, without the help of a salesperson. The relationship is simply a *transaction*, an exchange of goods for money. The best kinds of transactions are short and to the point.

In a transaction relationship, customers want an order taker and a price negotiator—not a salesperson.

Living and working in a world where prices and convenience are all that matters to the customer is not only tough on business, it is also punishing on everyone dealing with that customer. For example, one of our customers in the early 1980s was Moore Business Forms, which sold forms—invoices and traffic ticket blanks—to institutions. If you've ever received a speeding or parking ticket, it probably was written on a Moore Business Forms ticket.

Selling business forms was tough business in any case. Direct salespeople were the point people calling on purchasing agents of small and medium-sized companies. There was a lot of competition. Although the salespeople worked at establishing relationships with everyone from the receptionist and the purchasing agent, "relationships" was not what their customers cared about. They only wanted a nickel less per one hundred forms. If they couldn't get that from one salesperson, they would simply and easily switch vendors. The key words are "simply and easily switch."

For the salesperson, the day was made or broken by factors out of his or her control: the price, availability, and convenience of the product. Moore Business Forms was a classic commodities business, and 90 percent of its salespeople were calling on transaction buyers.

What does this have to do with your customers and your sales organization? In a world becoming more competitive every day, where new and powerful competitors appear routinely, every business faces the immediate threat of losing its differentiation in the eyes of its customers and becoming simply another vendor in the price and convenience transaction wars.

> "Today, in my industry there are fifty-six companies selling personal computers. And they are all the same, and they all look alike. Prices are pretty much the same. The customer expects service, so everyone delivers it. A high level of service is also becoming a commodity."
> — Tom Behr, Sales Manager, ISC-Bunker-Ramo, an Olivetti Company

It Is Simple and Easy to Switch

It comes down to switching cost—what does it cost a customer to switch from one vendor to another? The business strategy is, of course, to make sure that there is a high cost for the customer to switch to your competition. Customers factor in price, product advantages, service advantages, account longevity, and personal relationships when they consider switching or not. The more the cost to switch, the less likely they are to change suppliers.

✔ *How much would it cost your best customers to switch to your competition?*

✔ *What are "high switching cost" advantages that you have with your key customers?*

✔ *What are "high switching cost" advantages that your competitors have?*

✔ *How "at risk" are you for losing important customers?*

✔ *What are you going to do about it?*

To understand the potential crisis that lurks here for many organizations, stop seeing your marketplace through your company's perspective. It is the least appropriate, most biased perspective, the perspective that will most likely get you into trouble. Instead, put yourself behind the desks of your customers. They have three to five organizations (if not more) bidding on the business. The salespeople they are dealing with look alike, make the same promises, and can all do the same cost-benefit analyses. It is as if they all went to the same schools. Even the slick brochures that are left behind after the sales calls appear the same. Change the product names inside the brochures and you can't tell the products apart.

There is increasingly little difference, and it is simple and easy for that customer to switch vendors—it costs the customer very little.

> "All the banks in our market have exactly the same products, even the lobbies look the same. The switching costs are low. Customers will bank with us for a minute and then go over to Wachovia because they are paying a basis point higher. Differentiation from the rest of the pack is what drives our strategy."
> — Leslie Spencer, Vice President BB&T

As the world becomes smaller, the marketplace more competitive, business after business is waking up and finding itself figuratively stuck in this strange new swamp of the low-switching relationships and transactional buyers.

It can be a frightening wake-up call. A sales vice president for one of the large overnight package delivery companies gave this perspective. They have a capital-intensive business, airplanes, trucks, buildings, and a big international payroll. All of that is supported, of course, by thousands of packages flowing through their system every night. All of that is at risk because, as they have discovered recently, they live and die in a low switching cost commodity world.

All it takes is one competitor to undercut them by a few cents a pound, and the customers will switch and large chunks of market share will move with the switch. And the customers that will switch are customers that, by all measures, were satisfied customers.

Customer satisfaction is often misinterpreted as customer loyalty—it isn't! In a low switching cost world, where customer satisfaction is a given, a few pennies here, a few pennies there, make the difference. If you are on the wrong side of the pennies-per-pound equation, the business can begin to unravel quickly.

Sales management—the people usually directly responsible for increasing sales—are being hit by this low switching transactional environment. For sales management, this phenomenon brings into question the role of a salesperson.

✔ *What does the customer truly want from salespeople that we can realistically provide? How can salespeople create differentiation?*

✔ *What kind of training do they need?*

✔ *What kind of investments does the company need to make in the sales organization to make a difference for the customer?*

The Cost of Selling

But investing in a traditional, geographic "face-to-face with the customer" sales organization is a difficult proposition for companies today. The cost of that direct sales force is already skyrocketing. For example, a recent study done at Eastern Michigan State University found that when you add in all the commissions, travel and living expenses, benefits, and other expenses associated with selling, the total cost of salespeople runs an average of four times their base salary. A salesperson paid a base of $25,000 costs the company almost $100,000; a $50,000-base salesperson costs nearly $200,000.

COST OF INDUSTRIAL SALES CALL

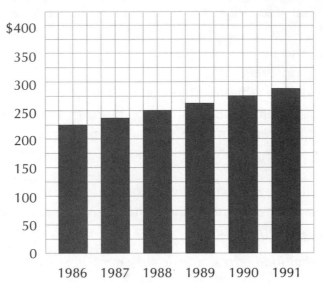

Source: *Sales & Marketing Management*

Another way to look at the same numbers is to consider the cost of a sales call. Over the past ten years, the raw cost associated with calling on customers has increased dramatically to nearly $400 per sales call.

Put all this together and you can see the dilemma. Organizations are paying higher sales dollars for a more volatile, less loyal, and more demanding customer. In economic terms, the return on a direct sales force is being hammered.

This issue became a matter of public record when a memo from IBM's former CEO John Akers was leaked to the press. In the memo, he raised hell over the return he was getting from adding five thousand more people to IBM's already overstaffed sales force. The year before, twenty thousand IBM salespeople had delivered $50 billion in sales. Akers added five thousand more salespeople and made *only $1 billion more in sales revenue*. He asked the question, "Who needs these guys?" Or, put another way, "Why should I add five thousand people to increase my sales $1 billion when twenty thousand salespeople are bringing in $50 billion? What kind of return on my investment is that?"

When IBM coughs, it's in the *Wall Street Journal*. But the same questions are being asked by companies all over the landscape. They are realizing that in the current low switching cost business environment, the costs associated with a traditional sales force are not worth the return. As a result, sales organizations in otherwise healthy companies are being slashed. Some have been eliminated in favor of alternative channels of distribution. Others are being downsized radically to focus on a smaller but more lucrative customer base. Most are experiencing ongoing reorganization as businesses strive to discover the mix that will best serve the customers of the nineties.

On the minds of executives—keeping them up at night—are some troubling questions: "Why do we need an expensive direct sales force in today's marketplace? Why do we need a large geographic sales force to take orders, explain pricing, and service accounts? *Do we need salespeople?*"

> "We don't need this damn big army any more. . . . We need to win with a third fewer people, fewer horses, fewer arrows and that strikes fear into hearts of major corporation people today."
> — Jim DeLong, Director of Sales, Miles, Inc., Agriculture Division

Yet there is more changing than just the economics of the business of selling. Technology is adding a brand-new spin to our profession.

Technosales

Here is an answer many sales managers and CEOs are using to solve the problem of the direct sales organization's being too expensive. They see all their transactional business being handled by a lower-cost, technology-driven group. The tools of this group are the telephone, the computer, and the fax machine. Technology is a large part of the solution in dealing with skyrocketing costs and transactional buyers. This shift is going on right now in all kinds of businesses.

A recent study published in *Business Week* estimated that 22 percent of the $29-billion-a-year personal computer and peripherals business is done by mail and telephone. This, incidentally, is the same computer power that only a few years back was the realm of the big mainframes sold by legions of salespeople in blue suits. The equipment usually arrives within two days, and prices are below those in retail stores. The lesson? Eliminate the direct sales force and associated infrastructure through the use of technology, and you can do some serious driving out of costs from the system.

If you're like me, you probably react strongly to this kind of information. If you're like me, you probably believe that nothing can replace the one-to-one relationship between a good salesperson and a customer.

I think that's still true—with some conditions. The conditions are what your customers want and need. Customers who want only price and convenience information probably don't need salespeople. Customers who know as much, or more, about your product or service as you do probably don't need a traditional salesperson.

For these customers, there are fewer expensive and more customer-focused approaches than a direct sales force. Innovations for meeting the needs of those customers are bubbling up all over the landscape.

Tele-everything

For example, there is a telesales revolution going on. By telesales, I don't mean those annoying aluminum siding sales calls that always happen while you're having dinner.

Rather, the shift is this: more and more industrial sales organizations are moving to telesales operations. Telesales are a large part of the answer to dealing with the transactional environment. It is less expensive and, paradoxically, more customer-focused, because it takes less time and can be controlled by the customer. Finally, in a transactional market, a telesalesperson can make upward of thirty contacts a day, compared with as few as three or four for a direct salesperson. To help understand this trend, we went to Gary Hultgren of Moore Business Forms and Systems Division. Gary was instrumental in that organization's move into the telesales arena.

"We started telesales in response to the wishes of our customers. They expected instant information and availability, and they were telling us we had to be quicker to respond. And sometimes the face-to-face sales call is not the answer. On the phone, the average sales call takes three to five minutes. There has never been a direct sales call made in that short a time.

> "Technology is critical to this entire undertaking. The days of manual anything in this type of operation are history. These organizations are fully automated and database-driven. Telesales are used for everything from servicing existing accounts to prospecting for potential customers."
> — Gary Hultgren, Director, National Telesales, Moore Business Forms and Systems Division

The growing acceptance of telesales is only one example of how technology is impacting sales. Computer linkups between supplier and customer allow products to flow to the customer as needed without order takers or phone calls. The ubiquitous fax machine transmits proposals, orders, and contracts anywhere in the world in minutes. And this is only the beginning. Information (the commodity we all deal in) will flow faster, more seamlessly, and less expensively than we can imagine, impacting everyone responsible for finding and keeping customers.

For example, the airlines' greatest competition in the coming decade will no doubt come from the telecommunication industry as video conferencing takes off and becomes an accepted—and less expensive—way of doing business. Recently, at our conference center in New Mexico, we put on thirty-five seminars, with one hundred salespeople per session, for a large organization. Senior management wanted to be involved in each session. But rather than fly out every other day, they set up an interactive teleconference link from their Chicago home office via satellite to the Pecos River Ranch. Senior management could see and hear the participants, and vice versa. Every other day, for thirty-five meetings, senior management was there "live" with every sales-person in the country. Technology is changing our future and will continue to pressure us to do business differently from the way we do it today.

Adding It All Up

Companies are paying increasingly expensive sales dollars for business at higher risk than ever before. Organizations are finding themselves in a low switching cost, highly competitive world. Further, customers have less time to see sales-people and, for a lot of organizations, technology promises a less expensive way of keeping in contact with the transactional market. Adding insult to injury, customers are more sophisticated, more knowledgeable than ever before and quite capable of making their own decisions between competing products or services without the assistance of sales-people. They just want prices faxed to them.

Put this all together and here is what emerges: the traditional sales model is beginning to creak and groan under the relentless pressure of permanent white water. Companies are waking up, realizing that they have a dinosaur for a sales organization, and that it is time for drastic measures.

All over the landscape, businesses are asking the same question: "Do we really need a sales force?"

For sales managers saddled with the responsibility of increasing revenue this poses a significant dilemma. The old solution was simply to hire more salespeople. But adding people to the payroll to chase after more revenue doesn't feel right to most sales managers in times of relentless cost pressures.

Another solution is to demand more production from a

smaller sales force, without changing the basic nature of how they sell. Ask any burned-out salesperson whose territory has been doubled, whose quota quadrupled, and whose actual time spent in front of the customer dropped by two-thirds if that can lead to success.

Competition, customers, and cost have decreed that the old game—the direct sales force out there knocking on doors, drumming up business, responsible for volume—no longer works.

So here are the questions: What will finding and keeping customers look like in five years? In ten years? Will we still "sell"? Will we still carry around in our heads the same knowledge and information? The answer is a resounding "No." The traditional business of customer finding, all those people out calling on customers and pitching product, is dead. They just haven't informed the patient yet.

We are being led—by customers, changing technology, and the requirement to be more productive—into a new world order of business.

Chapter Three

The Customer Has the Gun!

"Selling is a lot different now—a lot more fast and furious. When I started, there were fewer players and we all played the same game. It was "I get to win this one, you'll win that," and it was a big trade-off between a few major players. Now it's much more aggressive. A lot of very combative companies have entered the marketplace and changed the game with better prices, more delivery options, and more product-rich types of things. It's a furious market.

"Customers expect a lot more from the companies and the salespeople they deal with. They are more demanding, They are much more savvy about their alternatives and they are driving the business more than ever before."

— Tamae Moriyasu, salesperson,
Hewlett-Packard Company

Aggressive, fast, and furious—pretty good descriptions of what is occurring right now in that most critical of areas: the relationship between buyer and seller. That relationship, being fundamentally changed by the increasingly competitive and rapidly changing times we live in, is what we will explore next.

To understand the change, we need first to step back and understand the history of selling. When manufacturers had power by virtue of high demand and a constantly growing marketplace, selling was the business of persuading or inducing others to buy from you rather than your competitor. Careers were made or broken around the ability to motivate, cajole, influence, and otherwise convince buyers to go with you rather than the archvillain, your competition.

Playing the Roles

"The sales call" is like a classic film in which we know all the roles and can play them from memory. The opening scene begins with the salesperson sitting in the lobby waiting for the appointment, mentally playing self-made motivational speeches for himself or herself. "Go get him, Harry!" "He's got your commission check in his pocket!" "You can do it, just don't back down and don't forget to ask for the order!"

Then we cut to the customer and the salesperson in the office. The salesperson begins "relationship building," trying to find areas of commonalty, "So, Mr. Prospect, I hear that you're a big fan of the Minnesota Vikings. . . ." Cut to those all-important transition moments, where the salesperson begins the benefit statements: "Mr. Prospect, based on what you've told me, I really think that this model meets all your needs in terms of reliability and performance." Cut to the prospect objecting: "It looks like a very nice unit, but I'm afraid it is just not in my budget to spend that much money." The salesperson sees the commission check evaporating into thin air. "Uh, well, Mr. Prospect [How can you do this to me!], I understand your concern about the financial aspects, but maybe we can look at this a different way—I bet we can save you a lot over the lifetime of this model. And I am sure that I can get you a hefty discount, especially if we can work something out today."

Cut to the prospect nodding and the salesperson, mentally, of course, adding up that commission check. ("Yes! I can make the car payment!) Then, going for the big finish, the assumed close! "So, should I schedule delivery for Monday next or Wednesday?"

This drama is being played in every office building and on showroom floors every day. A salesperson attempting to sell a customer and the customer resisting, negotiating, determined to buy at a lower price. In the role of salesperson, we become competitive, determined to do whatever we can to make the sale, often without regard for the interests of the buyer. When we are cast in the role of customers, we, too, automatically resist being sold. We are naturally suspicious and wary. The supporting roles are those of sales management, putting pressure on the salesperson to sell more stuff, and the management of the buyer (or our spouses!) pressuring the buyer to stay on or below budget—not to be sold up the river, not to be taken for a ride.

This is the drama of selling, with the built-in conflict between buyer and seller, played over and over. Different industries, different companies, have their unique spins, but you can always recognize the play, the key players, and their roles.

Gun-to-Your-Head Selling

It was not always as subtle. It used to be more like a shoot-'em-up spaghetti western. Salespeople were taught that the customer was the enemy, not to be trusted. They learned how to "listen," that is, how to *pretend* to listen by nodding attentively while waiting only for the infamous buying signal. Salespeople were taught techniques to *overcome* objections and canned phrases to trap a buyer in a close.

The .45-Caliber Close

My favorite classic sales technique, dredged up from the bottom of the heap, was the .45-caliber close. A salesperson is sitting across the table from a prospect. The prospect is interested, but objects strongly to the price. The salesperson nods understandingly, then asks permission to ask a question. After the customer assents, the salesperson stands up, walks behind the customer, puts his index finger against the customer's skull, and says, "Imagine that I have a .45-caliber pistol pointed at your head. Would price still be a problem?" The startled customer replies, "No, of course not!" Salesperson: "So, then, what's the problem?"

Selling was *adversarial*. Salespeople were the hired guns, and the system was designed to support salespeople as they went out, banged on enough doors until they got a "yes," and then loaded the customer with as much product as possible. (For "product," fill in: insurance, computer hardware or software, medical supplies, or whatever your company sells.)

Selling was a hit-and-run business. Long-term relationships weren't developed, salespeople didn't care what business customers were in, as long as they had money they were willing to spend. With apologies to our distant ancestors, those were the Neanderthal days of selling. Although you still find pockets of that kind of selling, it was largely stamped out by sophisticated customers who would not tolerate that kind of abuse. In its place, selling evolved into a new and more customer-focused type of relationship called "problem solving."

I'm Here to Help!

Problem solving, currently the most common model for selling, is more customer-focused. The customer has a problem; the job is to help the customer *discover* what the problem is, and *solve* it.

Often salespeople spend a lot of time helping to invent the problem in the customer's mind. Remember the Broadway musical *The Music Man*? Harold Hill, the music man, first created a problem in the minds of the good people of River City. "Friends, you are not aware of the caliber of disaster indicated by the presence of a pool table in your community." Once that was firmly established as a problem, he pulled the solution out of his hat: a boys' band! Of course, the community slapped themselves on their collective forehead and said, "Why didn't we think of that?"

In the most refined version of problem solving, there is more focus on customers than on inventing pool table problems and band solutions. Salespeople with the best of intentions focus on solving their customers' true and actual needs. But meeting those true and actual needs revolves solely around product and price solutions—how my combination of product and price can solve your problem.

Yet, even in the most ideal problem-solving sales situation, that same drama is still being played out. The salesperson's job is still to sell the customer as much product as possible. Salespeople are not paid to solve customer problems, they are paid to sell products and services. If there is a connection between the problems and the product or service, great! But that is not what feeds the business. Volume is what feeds the business. And that is the eternal conflict.

Salespeople find themselves caught between the need to sell a product and solving a customer's true and real problems.

If you have any doubt about this, simply watch what happens at the end of the fiscal year. In a lot of organizations, the need to make sales heats up so much at year's end that customer focus takes a distant backseat. As the clock ticks down, product is loaded on customers, regardless of whether or not they need it. Sales management drives volume. Everyone focuses on the year-end numbers, not satisfying customers. Underneath the counselor attitudes and the "I'm here to solve your problem, Mr. or Ms. Customer" lurks the same adversarial spirit, simply dressed up in more sophisticated clothes.

In the past, in the more tranquil waters of higher demand than supply, organizations got away with this kind of selling, it was simply the way business was done. Today, like many formerly successful business patterns, this one is also creaking and groaning and beginning to fall apart. Why? Because the customer hates it—and the customer now can do something about it.

The fundamental premise of the old game, that you can sell someone something, is no longer true. Customers have always hated to be sold anything—they loved to buy, but they hate to be sold. Yet, for decades, customers have been shackled to this system of being sold. That was how the game was played. The selling organization had a lot of power; it was the way business was done. You might kick a truly repulsive salesperson out of your office, or walk out of a showroom. And the next salesperson might be a world apart in terms of personal style, but you knew he was there to sell you something. You knew that sitting on his shoulder were a sales manager, a company president, and stockholders, all whispering insistently in his ear, "Sell! Close! Get the check!"

> "I don't think anybody sells anything to anybody. I think people buy today—and that in itself is a huge difference."
> — Rick Canada, Director, Change Management Services, Motorola

More Choice + More Knowledge + More Sophistication = Power

The emerging customer, the undisputed master of the new business world order, is about to throw the old model of selling out on its ear. Customers are fed up with salespeople and organizations trying to sell them something. They're fed up, they're not going to take it anymore—and they no longer need to.

More Choice. Leading the list of causes is the fact that customers have more choices than ever before. Global competition, the commoditization of products and services, and the enormous price pressure that we previously discussed are all good news to your customers. It is no longer a matter of choosing between a few players. There are now hundreds of choices from all over the world—and that trend is certain to continue. From aircraft, to pharmaceuticals, to financial services, the world is shrinking and global competition is growing, all good news—to the customer.

More Knowledge. Customers have the knowledge to use that choice. Information is at their fingertips. There are no longer any secrets; customers can learn all about your industry and your business without ever leaving their offices. Instant electronic access exists to your annual reports and industry journals. Public companies are truly open and schoolchildren can find the salaries of corporate officers and who owns the stock, and examine a dozen Wall Street analyses of the financial health of the company—all on the home computer.

Information about your reputation, about how you treat other customers, flows in seemingly nanoseconds—to other customers and prospects. We are in the information age, on the entry ramp to the information highway. Knowledge is power—and customers are taking full advantage of it.

Ironically, selling organizations have helped create this highly informed and educated buying public to the point at which buyers are often better at buying than salespeople are at selling.

Word processing as a computer application is a good example. A word processing salesperson would come into a prospect's office and make the "concept sale." Lots of "oohs" and "aahs" about this new technology. The support people trained everybody, all the benefits were realized, and it was a big "win-win."

But the same supplier organization, coming back a few years later with the latest and greatest, runs into an entirely new buyer. That buyer—having been educated by the word processing sales and support organization—knows more about their specific applications than does the salesperson. The buyer also knows what the competition offers, what it would cost to switch, and what the downside is to your offering. That buyer is in the driver's seat.

> "I remember being trained to explain a system in terms of how much it cost per day over a period of time. Now, you would be laughed out of a customer's office if you tried to break it down to "Well, it's only five cents per second." Today, there is an expectation that you know more about their company, almost an expectation that you become part of their culture. They want you to understand what's driving their business, what goals they have as a company, and how your product fits in at that strategic level."
> — Tamae Moriyasu, salesperson,
> Hewlett-Packard Company

More Sophistication. The traditional game of selling has also run up against a customer that, beset by new high-level business problems, has become increasingly sophisticated and is demanding different kinds of solutions and support from supplier organizations. These new buyers are fluent in the world of Total Quality Management, Just-in-Time delivery, and out-sourcing. These buyers look at suppliers through a different pair of glasses, seeing them as critical to their business mission rather than as adversaries.

This new perspective stems from the work of the late, great Dr. Deming, who preached that true quality requires stopping the practice of buying on the basis of price alone. He also taught that working with fewer vendors in a close partnering relationship was one of the keys to quality and to driving cost out of the system.

Companies steeped in quality (and most are trying to get there) or in the idea of driving out cost are implementing Dr. Deming's mandates in a variety of forms. In this highly interdependent world, organizations realize that they cannot improve quality alone. Each part of the system, each company, each division, each individual, needs to contribute to quality and to driving out cost in order to truly make a difference. Large organizations are looking at their suppliers as key to their ongoing quest to improve.

Smart leading-edge companies, the ones who keep raising the bar on the rest of us, are already deeply involved in redefining their relationships with suppliers. Bob Gouin is manager of sourcing operations for General Electric Medical Systems in Milwaukee. GE Medical Systems manufactures diagnostic imaging equipment that is marketed globally. Bob is an industrial customer, responsible for buying approximately $1 billion worth of materials annually for his company's American manufacturing operations.

Bob is out to build new relationships with suppliers, to construct a sense of high-performing teamwork with the folks who were once considered adversaries. "We have what I call a 'strategic supplier initiative,'" he says. "Since 1988, we've reduced our supplier base from fifty-one hundred down to about thirteen hundred, selecting only those suppliers that we want to deal with long-term. This way, we can focus on total value instead of price buying."

GE is reinventing the relationship with its suppliers, moving it from adversarial to interdependent. Bob Gouin says, "What we're trying to do is develop an open and candid relationship with our suppliers. In the past, we held suppliers at arm's length. Now we want to bring them into the GE network, where we share technology and strategy."

This is a much more sophisticated customer than the traditional buyer of products and services. Supplier organizations, if they cannot work at this level, will be locked out, like the hundreds of suppliers that no longer work with General Electric Medical.

Think of it this way. Most of those organizations that formerly sold to GE had salespeople. Those salespeople either couldn't figure out what GE required or didn't move fast enough. But, more likely, the salespeople understood exactly what was going on. The salespeople went back to their companies and explained the new customer requirements and were told by their managements, "We don't do business that way" or "It isn't our policy" or "We can't share that kind of information with a customer." Management didn't understand how the customer was changing and how they need to change with the customer in order to keep the customer. As a result, they lost the business.

It is the customer's field, the customer's ball, and it is the customer's rules. Don't change with the customer, don't play the customer's game, and you won't play.

Power, Power, Who's Got the Power?

This is—ultimately—about power. The relationship between buyer and seller has always been about who has the power and how they use it to their advantage. As we've discussed, manufacturers, the suppliers of products and service to a growing and demanding marketplace, have traditionally held the power.

We are seeing a power shift all around from the manufacturer to the customer, from the supplier to the consumer. It is a shift that has been slowly going on for decades and it is now accelerating. The power shift is driven by the greater choice and knowledge of the customers.

In the words of the oft-quoted bank robber Willie ("Why do you rob banks, Willie?" " 'Cause that's where the money is") Sutton, "You can get more with a kind word and a gun than with a kind word alone." Now, the customer, who in the past relied more on the kind word, has the gun, and it's aimed at our heads.

> "Wal-Mart is the scourge of the earth, at least from the point of view of manufacturers who sell to Wal-Mart. Because Wal-Mart, as a customer, is taking control—power—away from the manufacturer. They do it with their scanning technology and bar-code tracking, which gives them specific information about what customers want. Wal-Mart turns around to the manufacturer and says, We want so much of this, packaged this way for this city, and for this city, something different. Manufacturing is losing control and manufacturers hate to lose control of the marketplace. It's driving us crazy. It costs big money. Manufacturers begin to wonder, Do we really want to do this? But on the other hand, do we have a choice?"
> — Jim DeLong, Director of Sales, Miles, Inc.,
>   Agriculture Division

The New Role of Finding and Keeping Customers

Whether your customer has more power than ever before, or is now looking for higher-level relationships, the consequences are the same: It is a new game of finding and keeping customers.

For example, tomorrow, or next quarter, can you create

the same kinds of relationships that Bob Gouin of GE talks about? What he is doing is going to be part of the new role for salespeople.

■ Tomorrow, could you help your best customer reduce cost without reducing your prices? Because that will be part of the role.

■ Tomorrow, will your company be able to share high-level information, resources, and people with your best customers? That will be an expectation.

■ Tomorrow, could you lead a team of people from your company and your customer's company through a comprehensive problem-solving process designed to impact high-level business problems? Because that will certainly be part of the job description.

Thriving in the marketplace of the nineties and beyond will require a new relationship between supplier and buyer. Remember, products and services are largely commodities, in your customers' eyes. Creating competitive advantage will need new solutions, new ideas, and new ways of working with customers. Having the best products or the most flexible pricing just gets you into the stadium. It doesn't get you onto the playing field anymore.

The same applies if your customers are looking for a relationship that can assist them with their quality or cost initiatives. If you're not willing to play that game, to understand your customers' larger needs, you will be passed over like the few thousand vendors who are no longer working with GE Medical.

The "finding and keeping customers" role is being transformed, and the leap we are about to take is necessarily large. We will have to leave behind many of our old beliefs, and our outdated policies. But the first part of the message is that we need to stop selling. We need to stop because, in its traditional adversarial state, selling is too expensive, it is punishing, and it simply doesn't work anymore. We need to stop selling because our customers no longer will tolerate it. They refuse to be sold, and what they are looking to buy often goes way beyond what exists in the briefcase of the traditional salesperson.

So here is where we are. All this change, all those dominoes that are causing the permanent white water, are now hitting where most companies live and die—in the relationships with their customers. But we have a choice. We can anticipate the future and change with it. Or we can put our heads in the sand, hope that everything "gets back to normal," and risk finding ourselves hopelessly locked out of the future.

That's the choice. That's where we are, and this is where the journey into the future begins.

Part Two

~~~~~~~~~~

Imagining the Future

"There is at least one point in the history of every company when you have to change dramatically to rise to the next level of performance. Miss the moment and you start a decline."

— Andrew Grove, CEO, Intel, in *Fortune*,
May 3, 1993

Revolutions create innovation and ideas. Revolutions are the birthplace of a new order, a new way of seeing the world, of thinking and working. From the fragments of the old order, people reassemble the pieces into something new and supremely fit for the revolutionary times. The pieces come together when people break with the past and imagine the future.

In this next part, we will collectively imagine the future of finding and keeping customers. What will the future be like if we can meet the needs of the emerging, tough, sophisticated customer? What will the future look like if we can create relationships that are successful, profitable, and sustain our businesses as well as our customers'?

The future is launched first in our imaginations, so imagine this: your best customers rave about you and your organization, they talk about you and your company as the way business should be done by everyone. Those same customers ask you to participate in their strategic planning sessions; they want your ideas on how—together with you—they can become more competitive. Imagine that as a result of these kinds of relationships, your business with these customers is profitable and secure. Imagine further that your company not only enthusiastically supports these kinds of partnerships, but also is organized to make them happen and sustain them for the long haul.

This part of the book is designed to help make these images of the future more concrete. We are going to look at what the future relationship between customer and supplier will be—a relationship we call "partnering." We are also going to look at what the customer-keeping organization looks like, the organization designed to create and maintain partnerships. Because when you boil it all down, keeping customers is critical: keeping customers is the mandate for everyone in the organization.

"Imagining the Future" continues the urgent theme of change: how all of us need to change in order to thrive in this new world. But be forewarned, change is difficult. Even when change is in our best interests, whether as individuals or organizations, we resist; we cling to habits of traditional ways of thinking and working.

Try this simple exercise. Cross your arms. Now put your arms down by your side and then cross your arms again— the opposite way.

If you are like most people, you had no problem crossing your arms your habitual way. After all, you've been doing it that way since you were a kid. You didn't have to think about it or plan it; it just happened. But when trying to cross your arms the opposite way—again, if you are like most people— it was a bit of a struggle. You had to think about it, it was even a bit embarrassing that you couldn't do it right away.

The point is that we are all—to greater or lesser degrees— creatures of habit, of comfort. We have built-in resistance to change. This resistance operates for individuals and for organizations.

This is the change conflict; even when change is in our best interests, we can find ourselves clinging to the past, to old beliefs—old ways of working. It blocks our ability to imagine a new future, grasp it, and make it happen.

The metaphor that captures this very human dilemma is that of the trapeze artist. In order to change, to grasp that future, we must first *let go* of the old trapeze, no matter how frightening that might be. We need to let go of the past, of the comfortable way of doing things, the traditions and the habits that we have grown accustomed to. We then go through a period of transition, temporarily suspended in midair while waiting for the next trapeze to show up. It's uncomfortable, and we often lose our bearings, our sense of where—and who—we are. Finally, we grab hold of the next trapeze and we are off to a new beginning.

Anytime we go through significant change, we go through all three stages—*letting go, transition*, and *a new beginning*. Since we are clearly going through revolutionary change, it is important that we be able to master change, to embrace it rather than be daunted by it. In this next part, we're first going to look directly into the heart of change, examining why we sometimes cling to the past and what is involved in letting go of it. Once we have let go of the past, with its assumptions about "the way things are," then the future can truly come alive with possibilities and potential. But first we have to let go of the old trapeze.

Chapter Four

Letting Go of the Trapeze!

> "This is an uncomfortable time. Even folks who think they'd like to change are finding themselves having to change beyond their paradigms. It creates a tremendous amount of insecurity."
> — Jim DeLong, Director of Sales, Miles, Inc., Agriculture Division

Over the course of the last decade, we have come to grips with the sense that tomorrow might not be like today, that tomorrow could possibly be the start of a journey where the destination is uncertain.

People who work in our economy—especially salespeople, who swim in the most uncertain of seas—are developing a higher tolerance for this ambiguity, for being willing to live and work with uncertainty and a touch of insecurity.

Of course, that is the way it has always been. All of our ancestors lived with uncertainty, chaos, and insecurity for countless generations. Only in this last flicker of a few decades have we been able to convince ourselves that life (and work) *should* be predictable, *should* be comfortable and safe.

Permanent white water has certainly broken that contract, fleeting as it might have been. In a real sense, what we are experiencing now is a large cultural wake-up call, telling us that change, uncertainty, and a touch of chaos are part of life and certainly the drivers of the next few decades. Since there is not much we can do to change that reality, we had best relearn how to thrive in uncertainty, how to exploit change, and take responsibility for our own futures.

Understanding Change

In 1986, when we believed that events were moving as fast as they possibly could, we wrote about understanding change in *Changing the Game: The New Way to Sell*. It described the three ways that individuals and organizations are brought to the point where they can overcome the forces of inertia, and change.

Crisis

The first cause of change is crisis. For organizations, crisis can be bankruptcy—as happened at Wang Labs—or suddenly realizing you are in a new marketplace with a slew of new competitors, a rapidly eroding market share, and plummeting profits. For the individual, crises may be divorce, being caught in a downsizing, or finding yourself as a salesperson with lots of new competitors in a new marketplace where your skills and assumptions no longer apply.

Adaptation

The next way to change is through adaptation or evolution. Someone tries something new, it works, and everyone copies it. The dealers of the GM spin-off, Saturn, introduced an innovative way of selling cars, and soon dealerships all over the country adapted by copying parts of the new way.

The cost of changing by adaptation, of course, is that you are perpetually number two, never the market leader.

Anticipation

The final way to change is by anticipation. You take the time and energy to see what the future will be; or you imagine the future you want and make it happen.

A classic example involves the VCR. An American company called Ampex invented the VCR technology. I remember buying one of their videotape recorders for a lot of money back in the late 1960s when my company, Wilson Learning Corporation, was preparing to go into video production as part of our training seminars. At that time, videotape recorders required a room full of equipment, specialists to run it, and miles of tape to record half an hour of video.

Ampex believed that the market for videotape recorders was the television studios and industrial TV production studios. After all, the machines were huge and expensive, and no one else could possibly afford them. And they were right—given that level of price, size, and complexity.

But what if they cost less than $500, were easy to use, and the size of a stereo? That is the question that another company, JVC, in Japan asked. JVC had a different approach to the same technological problem. When they studied the question, they saw a huge market, and that became their vision of the future. They worked on it for twenty years before they brought to market the first successful VCR.

Anticipating the future and changing to meet it are the proactive strategy—and obviously the one we believe is the way to success in the future. It requires a certain amount of risk, because you can be wrong. But to not play at all, to just wait and see what happens, is probably the more dangerous strategy. Change happens so fast that you cannot afford to be two or three moves behind the leaders. The marketplace is so competitive today that you can't afford to be satisfied with being third or fourth.

The seemingly safer, more secure strategy of changing by adaptation, by waiting until someone else figures it out, is no longer viable. The safe way has become too risky. In the unforgiving, permanent white water nineties, the ways to change are crisis and anticipation. Anticipation is a strategy. Crisis is, well, a crisis!

Letting Go of the Past

To anticipate requires, first, letting go of the past. But the past holds on to us and we hold on to the past. In a rapidly changing world, the beliefs and assumptions that made us successful in the past can turn rather quickly into serious misconceptions about what will lead to success in the future.

Remember the tale of Gulliver? He was the character who landed in the country of the tiny Lilliputians, fell asleep, and woke to find himself tied up by hundreds of invisible small ropes. There he was, a giant in the land of Lilliput, unable to move.

In the same way, we are all bound to the past by hundreds of assumptions and beliefs, many of them so much a part of us that they seem invisible. They show up in how we do business, or treat customers, or make assumptions about the future. For companies, these tiny ropes often take the form of policies and procedures that made sense at one time but are now hopelessly out of date—yet have never been changed because "that's the way we've always done it."

A woman who worked for a large client of ours told a story that emphasizes this point. Much of her old job was preparing a monthly report. She spent at least a full week each month in preparing the detailed written work, as she had for over a decade. She had inherited the report writing from the employee whom she had replaced. Well, one day, out of curiosity, she decided to find out where the report went and who read and used it. To her dismay, she discovered that no one read the report, and no one outside of her department was even aware that it was being produced. It was just something that had always been done. At some point in the last few years, the report became outdated, unnecessary, but the old behavior still continued because no one challenged the assumptions behind the status quo.

Left unchallenged, our assumptions can prevent us from anticipating the direction of the future; they can prevent us from recognizing that change is necessary. This happens at a personal level and a company level as well as at the level of nations.

For example, in the sixteenth century, there was a collective assumption, based on the best available evidence and general agreement about the way things are, that the sun and the stars revolved around the earth. That assumption fit all the observable data and seemed helpful in predicting the future, so no one challenged it—until an astronomer named Nicolaus Copernicus came along. He began to question the prevailing assumption. He examined the raw data in greater detail, using tools not previously available. Through more precise observation of the planets and the stars, Copernicus developed a theory that the earth revolved around the sun, and also rotated on its own axis.

Since this new theory completely contradicted the foundations of medieval science, religion, and philosophy, Copernicus was about as popular as a carrier of the black plague. In the medieval age, you didn't go up against prevailing wisdom, the map of the way things are, without severe consequences. Galileo, one of the few who agreed with Copernicus, was put on trial as a heretic for supporting "the false opinion that the sun is the center of the world and immobile."

For the crime of challenging the prevailing assumptions, Galileo was excommunicated. (And it took the institution that excommunicated him more than four hundred years to admit that he was right.) For the rest of the world, however, the Copernican theory was so powerful and compelling that it eventually prevailed against censorship and repression to become common knowledge. And, as time passed, it was modified and replaced by new theories and more accurate assumptions.

As businesses and as individuals, we are no different. We hold on to assumptions about how things are. Some of the assumptions are harmless, but others get in the way of our ability to see possibilities as the world changes.

A LITANY OF OLD ASSUMPTIONS

"Everything that can be invented has been invented."
>—Charles H. Duell, U.S. Patent Commissioner,
>   1899

"You ain't goin' nowhere, son."
>—Grand Ole Opry Manager to Elvis Presley, 1954

"There is no likelihood that man can ever tap the power of the atom."
>—Robert A. Millikan, Nobel Prize–winner in
>   Physics, 1923

"Heavier than air flying machines are impossible."
>—Lord Kelvin, President, Royal Society, 1835

"The Edsel is here to stay."
>—Henry Ford II, 1957

"Sensible and responsible women do not want to vote."
>—Grover Cleveland, former President, 1905

"Who the hell wants to hear actors talk?"
>—Harry Warner, Warner Brothers, 1927

Assumptions and Automobiles

This goes right to the heart of why it can be so difficult for large organizations to anticipate the future and change. Consider General Motors in the last two decades and the trouble they have had recovering from the oil shocks, the Toyota invasion, and their own internal quality and car safety short-comings. The root source of the problems of GM lies in the beliefs and assumptions of generations of managers, who, prior to the seventies, ran the largest and most successful corporation the world had seen. James O'Toole, professor of management at the University of Southern California, studied GM's leaders in the 1970s. He attended their meetings, interviewed managers, and researched the company. As a result of his extensive work, he developed a list of operating assumptions, the underlying beliefs and understandings shared by GM senior managers in the 1970s:

■ Managers should be developed from the inside.

■ GM is in the business of making money, not cars.

■ Success comes not from technological leadership but from having the resources to quickly adopt innovations successfully introduced by others.

■ Cars are primarily status symbols. Styling is therefore more important than quality to buyers who are, after all, going to trade up every other year.

■ The U.S. car market is isolated from the rest of the world. Foreign competition will never gain more than 15 percent of the domestic market.

■ Energy will always be cheap and abundant.

■ Workers do not have an important impact on production or product quality.

■ The consumer movement doesn't represent the concerns of a significant portion of the U.S. public.

■ The government is the enemy. It must be fought tooth and nail every step of the way.

■ Strict, centralized financial controls are the secret of good administration.

Reading that list in the light of the last two decades makes it seem pretty foolish. But it wasn't foolish; it was a powerfully successful view of the way things were in 1970. The assumptions fit all observable data and were helpful in predicting the short-term future. Remember, in those years, GM was so big, so successful, that the United States Congress considered breaking up the company. We should all be so successful! So this is not about taking potshots at GM. It is about understanding how powerful assumptions are and how they can act as blinders to the world changing around us.

✔ *Are you running on old assumptions and beliefs?*

✔ *Are they assumptions about the world and the marketplace, which, while successful in their day, are now inaccurate?*

The GM assumptions are an example of the trap each of us—individual or corporation—can easily fall prey to, especially if we've been successful. It is an easy one to fall into, this trap of clinging to the comfortable past, ignoring change, and hoping that things will just get back to normal soon.

Understanding our present beliefs and assumptions is such an important part of being able to change that we begin many of our programs at Pecos River Learning Centers by having the participants describe their current assumptions about business and selling. What mind-set do they go to work with every day? What are the unshakable assumptions they hold—like the "fact" that the sun revolves around the earth?

Some of the assumptions we've heard are as follows:

We assume . . .
We know who our customers will be.
Future customers will always look like current customers.
Customers will always need our current products.
Customers need us more than we need them.
Customers are all alike.

We assume . . .
There will always be commissioned salespeople.
Money is the way to motivate reps.
Full commission sales reps are the way to go.
Money equals happiness for reps.

We assume . . .
Competition is not a big factor.
Our competitors are our enemies.
Our competition will not change dramatically.
We have no natural competition.

We assume . . .
Bigger is better.
Communication between the top and the field force is not
    important.
Marketing strategies will always be successful because the
    top has the answers.
Management skills come naturally; managers don't need
    training.
Managers can save accounts in trouble.

We assume . . .

Personal selling will always be important.

Relationships are critical to the sale.

Sales will always sell and service will always support.

Salespeople need to know everything about their products.

Sales have to be conducted face-to-face.

You need to give customers "perks" to keep the business.

Customers will continue to buy from those they know and
like.

How many of these assumptions will seem just as foolish
in a few years as General Motors' assumptions from 1970?
Will we look at them some day and think, "How could we
have been so wrong?"

The only way to avoid colliding with old assumptions is to
constantly challenge them, especially the old truths, the unspoken business axioms. This necessitates asking uncomfortable questions like "Why do we do business this way,
exactly like our competitors? Why are we organized the way
we are? What do our customers really want?"

Challenging the prevailing "way things are" often means
taking risks, trying new things, making mistakes, even failing. It takes courage. It can mean risking the disdain of your
peers, even risking "excommunication" from your organization.

So why take the risk?

The Mattress Express

Fair question. Because if we don't take risks, we may find
ourselves, someday soon, out of business, overwhelmed by
competitive forces and throwing up at the side of the road.

Glen Grodem, president and CEO of the Portland-based Smith Home Furnishings, told us this story. Smith Furnishings retails refrigerators, home electronics, and home computers. Smith has grown from $40 million in sales in 1986 to $240 million in 1992.

Their story about challenging assumptions and anticipating the future concerns one of the lowest of low-tech businesses: mattresses.

Buying a mattress, for most, unfolds like this: over the years, people notice that their mattress is deteriorating. Then, one day backs seriously begin to hurt, there is lots of tossing and turning, and soon the mattress commercials on television begin to make sense. An average of two weeks after that, the committed, cash-in-hand mattress buyers finally come into a store to buy a mattress. In their mind, they've had back pain for two weeks, the old mattress is to blame and they want a new mattress and the pain gone—now.

What happens next? The "I want it now" buyers run into the unchallenged industry assumption—a one- to two-week wait for delivery. It is how business has always been done. For customers, that means at least one more week of back pain. For Smith Furnishings, it meant an opportunity.

"Mattress delivery was kind of a sleepy business. It took an average of four to five days to deliver a new mattress and no one ever bothered to haul away the old mattress. That was a major problem for people. Who wants an old mattress in front of your house?

"At the same time, I heard about this idea from one of

the best retailers in the country, Art Vann in Detroit. So I bought his idea, enhanced it with ideas from our research, and launched Mattress Express. First, we guarantee delivery of the new mattress within twenty-four hours, seven days a week, including Sundays. Second, we promise to haul away your old mattress. If we don't do either, your new mattress is free.

"It was an extremely successful idea. We took market share overnight from most of our competitors."

— Glen Grodem, President and CEO,
  Smith Home Furnishings

Smith Home Furnishings challenged the underlying assumptions of the traditional mattress business, benchmarked a good idea, and created the future of that business in their marketplace. And it changed the business.

Because Smith Home Furnishings anticipated and created the future, most of their competitors had to adapt or risk going out of business. Other competitors experienced crisis.

"The day we launched our Mattress Express radio and print campaign, the merchandising manager of one of our big department store chain competitors was driving home from a vacation with his family. He heard the radio spot, pulled his car over to the side of the road, got out and was sick. He knew he had just lost the mattress business. And he was right!"

— Glen Grodem

Throwing up on the side of the road. That is what we mean by crisis!

The Mattress Express story illustrates the choice most of us face: change by anticipating or change by crisis. We can anticipate the future, or we can find ourselves throwing up by the side of the road because we suddenly ran into the future that someone else—our competitor—created.

The Business Adventure

The choice to change inevitably requires doing the tough work of ruthlessly challenging assumptions, challenging our beliefs about the way things are. Whether you are a billion-dollar organization or an individual, you can't move into the future until you are willing to relinquish the past, to let go of the old trapeze.

Is there risk involved in all of this? Of course. Are there factors out of control? Absolutely. Creating the future is an adventure—remember, the outcome is uncertain. But certainty and "risklessness" have never existed. They are simply made-up assumptions that aren't very useful.

> "Security is mostly a superstition. It does not exist in nature. Avoiding danger is no safer in the long run than outright exposure. Life is either a daring adventure or nothing."— Helen Keller, American educator

You can disagree vehemently with everything that lies ahead in this book. After all, the next couple of chapters simply are our best thinking about the future of finding and keeping customers.

But the caution flag here is this: do not allow yourself to believe that you have it all figured out. Don't get comfortable. Do not allow yourself to believe that because you are highly successful today, your success formula will still be working next year or in five years. There is simply too much "rattling and shaking" going on.

In business, we are each responsible for creating our future. It starts with challenging our assumptions and deeply understanding our customers' needs—plus a little intuition and foresight. Obviously, a little luck will help. The next few chapters will give you something to think about, but, ultimately, it is up to each of us to create our future.

■ What are your assumptions (the underlying unchallenged beliefs) about:

   Your customers?

   Your business?

   What your business will be like tomorrow, or next year, or in five years?

■ What information do you have about the present and future that contradicts your assumptions?

■ Based on the information, which of your assumptions are outdated, no longer true? Which need to be examined more carefully?

Chapter Five

Married to the Customer

What does the future look like? What kind of relationship is required to find and keep the emerging customer of the future?. Lou Pritchett, the former VP of worldwide sales for Procter & Gamble, has not only seen that future but has also helped create it. Lou and I first met in 1987, when I spoke to his sales group at Procter & Gamble. Since retiring from P&G, Lou has become a sought-after speaker in his own right, with audiences hanging on his every word, because Lou has been there. In his words, he has "carried a bag" as a salesperson for P&G and has also seen the business from the eagle's nest as the vice president of worldwide sales.

Audiences are captivated by Lou because he has such a clear grasp of the future of selling. Thirty minutes with Lou, and you are ready to go out and slay dragons, reorganize companies, and completely redefine the idea of working with customers. That's Lou Pritchett.

To hear Lou tell it, his awakening began in the early 1980s, when he became president of Procter & Gamble Philippines. When he arrived in the Philippines, the company had lost market share and its number-one position vis-à-vis the competition. Lou dug into the business, discovering problems such as huge unsold inventories and a factory-out, "keep shipping product" mentality that kept perishable products like toilet soap in warehouses for up to six months in 110 degree heat and 90 percent humidity, "lathering like a slick rock." This created a very expensive problem for P&G and its customers. But the mentality of the Philippine company at that time was to generate volume, keep shipping, and never, ever run out of product.

One of Lou's first actions—which sent shock waves up and down the Procter & Gamble pipeline—was to declare a moratorium on selling and shipping product. Next, and probably for the first time in the history of P&G Philippines, he went out and interviewed his customers.

"I started doing focus groups with customers," says Lou, "and it was amazing. They talked and I listened. They knew what our problems were. But we had never asked them for help. So I started asking, 'What should we do?' And they told me, 'We should work together like brothers. If I know your business and your problems, I can help you. If you know ours, you can help us.'

"As a result, I started thinking that we had to completely change the way we go to market. We had to move away from the short-term, volume-moving mentality. We had to really align with customers and create partnerships."

As a result of this new understanding and other changes, within two years, Lou's group in the Philippines recovered lost market share and regained its paramount position in sales and profits. P&G then brought Lou back to fight other dragons as vice president, sales. And Lou again began to make waves. Once again, he started by going out and interviewing customers.

"When I took the idea to my bosses," Lou recalls, "they were nervous; they worried that some customers would try to take advantage of us. But as I did the interviews, those folks didn't ask for a thing. They loved P&G. In the spirit of telling the truth, they also helped me understand the problems that made it sometimes difficult for them to do business with us. For example, one customer told us that they kept an accountant working simply to decipher the various P&G contracts.

"My favorite story—a turning point for me and the one that really woke me up—was about a big Bounty towel promotion sale at a Boston chain. It was scheduled for Thursday, but as of 3:00 P.M. Wednesday, not one single truck or rail car had arrived. At 4:00 P.M., the manager's assistant came in and said, 'There's a Procter & Gamble guy in the waiting room.' The manager ran out of his office and embraced the salesman, saying 'Thank God, you're here!' He poured his heart out and then this salesman took two steps back and said, 'Sorry, sir, I'm in the toothpaste side of the business.' "

As anyone who has tried it knows, you don't change the direction of the ship simply by memo or exhortation, even if you are the vice president of sales. This is especially true when the ship is a huge, traditional, successful 150-year-old corporation. Lou knew that he needed a big win, a big idea. So he did his research and discovered that Wal-Mart was P&G's largest customer. He further discovered that, although ten to twelve divisions of P&G were calling regularly on Wal-Mart, it was a totally uncoordinated effort.

Lou continues: "I learned a very startling fact: P&G's largest customer had never been called on by a senior P&G officer. So I picked up the phone and called Sam Walton. I told him we should get together and talk because our companies were going in opposite directions, which was expensive for both of us. That got his attention, because he had two basic goals: to empower people, and to drive excess costs out of the system without passing them on to the consumer.

"Well, Sam said that he'd love to talk but that he didn't do business very well in his office. So we ended up going on the now-famous canoe trip on the South Fork River in northeastern Arkansas. It was on the river that Sam and I came to the realization that our two very large, complex, and sophisticated companies were communicating with each other by slipping notes under the door. We were two entities burdened by—but oblivious to—the excess costs created by this obsolete system.

"We realized that, in order to thrive in the future, we had to break away from the short-term adversarial confrontation of win/lose which had been the hallmark of the past twenty years and move toward a partnership built on trust and committed to a vision. Not our vision, not their vision, but a shared vision. We had to change the system together."

As a result of their trip down the South Fork, Sam Walton and Lou Pritchett brought together the top ten officers from both companies to work on developing this new relationship. Within three months, they had created and empowered a multifunctional P&G/Wal-Mart team. P&G initially relocated twelve people to Bentonville, Arkansas, Wal-Mart's headquarters. That number eventually grew to more than seventy-five.

According to Lou, the high-level communication, the aligning of systems, the reduction of inventories, and so on, have led to double-digit growth for both companies in the affected product lines. This relationship, which went beyond any sales or contractual relationship previously held by P&G, profoundly influenced the thinking of both companies. In a letter to Lou, Sam Walton wrote, "I think back on our first canoe trip and how we evolved the partnership process with P&G. It was one of the best things that ever happened to our company."

The key was that they both knew that the traditional relationship between buyer and seller, and all the historical baggage that came with it, was antiquated, expensive, and out of touch with current reality. It took two high-level, experienced individuals who were comfortable bucking "the way things are" to launch this new relationship. They approached the situation not from a product and service point of view but from a different vantage point: How can we together drive cost out of this relationship so that we can both win? Finally, they approached the problem together, as collaborators in a true partnership. Lou says:

"Whenever tough times come, people stand down and reflect. Management is now standing down and realizing that the old nonaligned confrontational systems are simply not working, and that we cannot continue to go through this transactional process to prove that my product, price, or service is better than my competitor's. It is very, very costly and counterproductive.

"What they are thinking about is this: What if our customers wanted to do business with us because they saw the benefits at a high level? What if they saw that we can help them drive costs down, that we want to cooperate and not confront? What if our systems became compatible instead of butting heads? I think management is beginning to see that, just as in marriage or friendship, cooperation always beats confrontation."

Lou Pritchett is pointing the way to the future, to relationships that go beyond solving problems with products and services, that result in businesses coming together in more meaningful ways.

Partnering

Married to the Customer

To clarify the difference between partnering and other business relationships, think of a marriage. Granted, not all marriages are healthy, and you wouldn't want to model a business relationship on a bad or even mediocre marriage. But a significant minority of marriages have a lot to teach us about Lou Pritchett's vision of partnering.

After all, a relationship, whether between two individuals or two large organizations, is a connection, an alliance made strong or weak by similar forces and constraints. So think about a strong marriage. What are its characteristics?

First of all, it is *long term*. The healthiest marriages last a lifetime. They do so because each partner is committed to the other, each one trusts, and has deep, abiding love and respect for, the other. They have ups and downs, good times and bad (the vows are for better or for worse), but they stick together because the relationship is built on a solid foundation.

The foundation of strong, long-term marriages is made of similar values and the same world view. The partners share a common, elevating purpose—to raise happy and ethical children or to build a life together. The marriages that we would all like to emulate are built on equality; each partner is respected by the other for his or her talents, for what each brings to the table. If the partners work at it, a marriage evolves to a state of interdependence—a unique combination of independence and dependence—that is healthy enough to last a lifetime. These are the rare, wondrous relationships—and the same principles apply to partnerships.

Partnerships are:

■ Long term (in business, long-term means three to five years, or more).

■ Business-focused—focused on solving important business problems, rather than simply selling products.

■ Value-driven—high levels of disclosure, trust, truth, and support.

■ Interdependent—there is a variety of connecting points between organizations, a blurring of the lines between organizations.

Strategic and Value-Driven

The ability to solve high-level business problems is the reason buyer and supplier come together in partnerships. It used to be that products or price drove the relationship; the person who had the best product or the best price got the business. That is no longer a reliable rule. In today's highly competitive commodity world, there are rarely competitive differences between suppliers; if there are distinguishable differences, they are short-lived.

To raise the bar, to stay competitive in this new world, the most sophisticated organizations and salespeople have discarded traditional notions about what drives the relationship between buyer and seller. Products don't give competitive advantage. Value-added service is now an expectation. So what is left? What can you provide?

The new game is based on the ability to help solve significant business problems for customers. If you want to play,

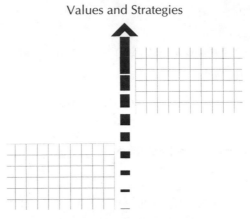

Values and Strategies

Tactics and Products

competitive advantage lies in helping your customers make money, save money, or add value to *their* customer.

The implications for supplier organizations are this: building competitive advantage solely around products and services isn't enough. Understanding your *customer's* business, strategy, market forces, and financial situation is the new core competency.

✔ *What are your customer's goals?*

✔ *How do they make money?*

✔ *What can you do to help them expand their business?*

✔ *Who are your customer's customers?*

✔ *How can you help add value to your customer's customer?*

Shared Values

Of course, no person or organization is going to let you in the door, make you privy to their critical business issues, unless they trust you and are confident that you share their basic beliefs regarding business, their values.

Think of it this way. As a customer in a transactional environment, all I wanted was for you to drop the product off on the loading dock. Your values were not that important to me. Honesty and fair pricing were expected. At this higher level, however, more is required. Both organizations and the individuals involved need a higher level of commitment to a partnership. The deeper and more interconnected the relationship, the more trust and values play a critical role. For example, if proprietary information is shared or products are developed in common, everyone needs to feel confident that the same information will not be shared with competitors.

These relationships are often more akin to hiring a new employee than they are to working with a new vendor or a new customer. When an employee is hired, there is an expectation that at some level, he or she will share the core values regarding work, people, and ethics that are expressed by the company and that are shared by other employees. A partnership requires the same level of disclosure, discourse, and discovery.

✔ *What are the expressed values of your best customers?*

✔ *What do they hold as important? What do they look for in new employees? Why do they fire people?*

✔ *What are your values? What are your business priorities? What do you hold important?*

✔ *Based on the above, where are the value matches and where are the value conflicts?*

Interdependent: From Me to We

> "The best definition of a partnership I can think of is when the buyer and the seller take on the characteristics of one organization, rather than two separate, distinct organizations."
> — Rick Canada, Director, Change Management Services, Motorola

The next dimension of the relationship concerns how we work together and who is involved.

The adversarial nature of selling seems part of our culture, part of the essential nature of the relationship. Yet, for those who can break through this old and punishing paradigm— both customers and suppliers—the result can be a significantly enhanced relationship.

This shift is from adversarial to interdependent, from "me" to "we." With that shift comes a blurring of organizational boundaries. The question "Whom do you work for?" becomes harder to answer. In this interdependent world, sales and service people work in their customer's location. Customers sit on supplier teams. Everyone is focused on the same task.

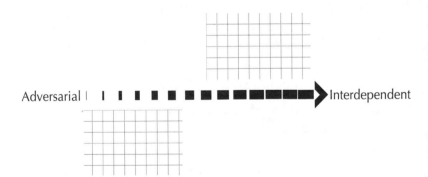

Adversarial ⟶ Interdependent

Who Is Involved?

The simple answer is: every part of the organization. Partnering transforms the relationship from just a single or a few points of contact (salesperson to buyer) to multiple points of contact between the organizations.

The implications for salespeople as relationship managers are clear. In order to manage these new relationships, the "partnership builders" will require a high degree of integrity and new competencies, like the ability to work at the highest levels of customer organizations, the skills to facilitate groups, and a deep understanding of organizational dynamics.

Putting It All Together

Strategic, value-based, and highly interdependent: these are the characteristics of the partnering relationship that make it the business equivalent of those long-term, special marriages. Like marriage, partnering is not appropriate for everybody. Many customers prefer to work with the low-cost providers; they will be commodity-type customers forever. But the emerging, sophisticated customers, the customers of world-class organizations, are looking for organizations and individuals with whom they can partner to do serious business, because of the enormous rewards to be reaped.

Lou Pritchett is certainly one of the parents of partnering. He saw a new relationship between buyer and seller based on collaboration and trust instead of the adversarial relationships of the past. But take Lou's vision a step further—what will business relationships of the future look like as the world becomes increasing more complex and collaborative?

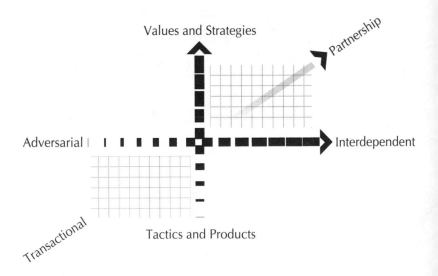

The Future of Business

Meet US West's Phil Styrlund, the director of strategic accounts for the Business and Government Services Market Unit in Minneapolis, Minnesota. Phil is responsible for US West's top eleven corporate clients in the Twin Cities.

> "I believe in my heart and in my mind that the only viable, sustainable future business model is one of collaboration. In almost every market today, the competitive dynamics and the global economic system are simply too complex for any single player to bring all the core competencies needed to the marketplace. The future will require alliances, often with companies that were formerly competitors. For example, players A and B competed in the computer market and always competed against each other. This is old-world thinking. Today, collaboration and competition co-exist in relation to the market requirements. Today, you may compete in the morning with a company and collaborate with them in the afternoon."
>
> — Phil Styrlund

Sustainability

Driving Phil's thinking is sustainability—how to create highly profitable business relationships for the long term. To Phil's way of thinking, anyone can create short-term results; the right combination of price, products, and service will give competitive advantage, but only for the moment—until your competitors copy it down to the last detail, which can happen overnight.

"Products are not the future. Services are the future. Painfully, almost any product that can be produced can now be rapidly replicated in today's world. Anything and everything is a commodity. The only sustainable difference is the ability to wrap services around a product to create something synergistic—greater than the sum of its parts. This is where partnerships come in to play. Different organizations collaborating to focusing their core competencies on well-defined market groups—that is how we will create the service and product solutions of the future."
—Phil Styrlund

Creativity from Diversity

The old business model of supplier and buyer was this: you were in your business and I was in mine and there were clearly defined boundaries between us. Your product was shipped to our loading dock and we used that product to help us create a solution, defined solely by us, for our customer. We rarely shared anything but invoices and Christmas cards. When we did talk, it was to solve the mundane problems like billing errors. We never shared our intellectual capital, we never, ever shared our product development ideas or where we were going in the future. In fact, in many companies, employees could be fired for talking about future product development with a customer—or a supplier.

Phil Styrlund and others are breaking up this mold and creating relationships that bring the maximum intelligence, creativity, and resources together from all stakeholders to create solutions for the customer.

Phil is anticipating markets that today do not exist: What

are the products and solutions that consumers will need in the future, that are not even being imagined today? As Phil points out, products like the Sony Walkman, the minivan, the Macintosh computer—none of those were created by reacting to what customers wanted, none were created in consumer focus groups. Most of us using cellular phones or voice mail today had no idea ten years ago that they would be required to do business in the nineties, that they would be an assumed part of the daily landscape. These solutions were created in the minds and imaginations of individuals anticipating the direction of markets, not reacting to them.

Diversity from Partnerships

The key to creativity is diversity—lots of different perspectives and ideas all directed at solving the problems and anticipating the solutions in a market. The more ways a problem is seen, the larger and more varied the perspective, the larger and more interesting the solutions,.

Diversity requires exploding—figuratively—the company, getting outside the traditional boundaries and barriers and bringing in the market intellect of all the players, suppliers, manufacturers, and customers.

For example, someone soon will create a bank card/ cellular phone combination. (I have no idea what we'll do with it, but if it saves time and makes life more convenient, we will all see it as a necessity.) It won't be a telecommunications company nor will it be a financial services corporation that creates such a solution, it will be a partnership that can create solutions that are greater than what would have been created separately.

"If the intellectual and market intuition of the partnership you are creating isn't greater than the sum of its parts—don't do it."— Phil Styrlund

Prescription for Partnership

We asked Phil to walk us through his phases for creating partnerships. What had to be in place for the relationship to be successful? He started by talking about *personal readiness*. The individuals involved, not just the companies, had to be ready to work at this higher level of complexity, reward, and risk.

In a serious partnership, for example, US West might partner with a bank to run their telecommunications division. That is a US West core competency and it may not be a core competency of the financial institution. The risk for the bank employees is, of course, their jobs. Even though it makes sense for the bank, the employees could soon find themselves reporting to their former supplier or even working for US West. Those individuals risk having their jobs redefined or occasionally lost. Yet, in the struggle for competitive survival, the bank needs to explore the options and their employees need to be willing to take the risks to create those kinds of solutions, embrace them, and make them succeed.

Phil's next prescription was *organizational readiness*. The organization has to be open and structured to receive and nurture partners, be they supplier partners or customer partners. The organizational immune system—which attempts to kill anything that is strange and new—has to be switched off in order to accept new relationships.

All the organizations in the partnership need to be in alignment, with lots of communication, shared vision of what is possible, and shared goals. The top executives have to be in agreement and support the principles of the partnership.

The next crucial part of a partnership is *clear milestones*. As Phil has experienced it, sometimes there is a tendency in the early part of the partnership to pull up the roots to see if it's growing—which, of course, can kill the partnership. There needs to be discipline and agreement around indicators. Like a marriage, partnerships are created for long-term advantage and they often need time to flower and grow.

Finally (just like in a marriage), all the parties need training and tools in *conflict resolution*. How do we agree to disagree? How do we agree to solve our problems together? For example, we agree to trust each other's intentions regarding the partnership, no matter the depth of the disagreement. In that sense, a partnership is a boat. Disagreeing and arguing is permissible, it is healthy, it doesn't put serious holes in the boat. Questioning the intentions of others in the partnership is putting holes in the boat below the waterline—it will sink the boat.

Phil's prescription for partnering—especially the personal and the organizational readiness to partner—is a prescription for how we will do business in the future. It describes the new relationships and abilities that we will all participate in (sooner, hopefully, rather than later) because there is so much to be gained.

Communities of Organizations

Take this to the next level and you can begin to see how business will be organized in the next century. Imagine communities of organizations, all working together with high levels of collaboration and inventiveness to create new solutions and serve new markets. Imagine that in this community of organizations, the boundaries are so blurred that employees are working for one company one year and another the next, and a third the following year—all the while working on the same project and receiving the same paycheck.

In this imagined future, organizations are open structures, partnering with whoever is best suited to bring solutions to a market and then moving on to create new partnerships and new markets. In this new order, collaboration, risk taking, strategic thinking, and creativity all become what is required for organizations and the individuals of the future.

"The key idea is this: The only *sustainable* successful business model for the future is a deep collaboration that aligns core competencies of organizations, that creates intellectual diversity to anticipate not only the markets of the present but also of the future. That's the model."
— Phil Styrlund

Fast Forward from the Past to the Future

Clearly, there are a lot of Lou Pritchetts and Phil Styrlunds out there creating these new partnering relationships. To a great extent, they represent the practices of generations of the best salespeople.

"A lot of very experienced salespeople were out creating partnerships with customers twenty-five years ago when I was on the road selling. We didn't call it a partnership at the time, but it was a caring, sharing, cooperative, trusting relationship where we said, If you cooperate with me, I'll cooperate with you. If we empower those people who are out there where the action is, I think they will tell us what partnering is all about and what we need to do to get there quickly."— Lou Pritchett

The Key Word Is "Quickly"

Events are moving so fast today that we cannot wait to adapt someone else's idea. There isn't the competitive window of time to study something, or wait until it becomes accepted best practice.

Many healthy partnerships are monogamous—they are single-source relationships. The costs of switching from a working single-source relationship to someone else are exceptionally high; competition is locked out.

A metaphor: Have you ever seen a time-lapse film of water freezing on a small pond? The ice crystals spread over the surface of the lake, hardening, squeezing out the water, until there is nothing left but ice. In that same way, suppliers and buyers in every industry are linking up, making stronger connections, squeezing out the weaker players.

The future of the buyer-seller relationship is rapidly moving toward partnering. We can wait for the crisis—being locked out—or we can anticipate and begin creating this future with our best customers.

Chapter Six

〰〰〰〰〰

The Customer-Keeping Company

Every once in a while, I like to get off airplanes and travel by train. It's a chance to see the country, to slow down, and to read a couple of good "whodunits." In that spirit, a few years ago, my wife and I decided to return to Santa Fe from Los Angeles by train. We had been working on the road for days, it was soon to be Thanksgiving and I needed a break. I had a vision of relaxing on the train, rocked to sleep by the gentle rhythm of the rails, and waking up refreshed as the spectacular beauty of the New Mexico desert and mountains unfolded outside the window.

We boarded the train in Los Angeles at 8:00 P.M. and headed east. True to my vision, we were both asleep immediately after dinner.

Well, we did go east, but not quite as far as we had planned. Around midnight, the train stopped and we were told that, due to a mechanical problem, our car was being uncoupled from the rest of the train and we would have to get off. We were all sleepy and cold; it was the middle of the night, and we had no idea where we were. So much for the romance of rail travel.

Understand that the problem wasn't that there was a problem. Problems happen, trains break down, equipment doesn't work as promised, people make mistakes, customers get upset. Perfection is the goal, not reality. It's *how problems are dealt with* that provides insight into a company, be it the train company or your company.

Out there in the middle of nowhere, our conductor's priority was to get us off the train and into the hands of the stationmaster as quickly as possible. He went so far as to tell us flat out that his responsibility was moving the train, not dealing with customers (especially *upset* customers).

As we watched the train disappear into the darkness, our hopes turned to the person who was supposed to be in charge of customers, the stationmaster. As it turned out, a bad choice. For the next two hours, the abandoned passengers argued with the stationmaster about what to do. The station-master's vocabulary was limited to one word— "No"—and his actions limited to calling his supervisor. We asked him to make cab, hotel, and airline reservations for us. No, not without permission from the higher-ups.

At long last, they agreed to pay for cab fare, hotels, and airfare to our various destinations. Receipts were made up and the travelers lined up to collect their refunds. Just when we thought this customer service nightmare was over, the stationmaster informed us that he didn't have enough money to refund the tickets!

It's easy to get mad at such employees, to blame them. We have all fumed or yelled at customer service people and, in turn, no doubt been yelled at by our customers (what goes around, comes around). But rarely are the employees the villains. More often, they are following the rulebook, following the orders—explicit or implicit—of management. In this typical customer relations screwup, the employees were following management's rules:

Rule No. 1. *Employees shouldn't think for themselves (because they can't).*

Rule No. 2. *Customers are the enemy and are never to be trusted.*

The train employees in this story were simply behaving in a way that was consistent with the company's mind-set. They were serving their boss.

The district supervisor's—the stationmaster's boss—attitude clearly sums up the train company's beliefs about customer service. When we asked to just speak to him on the phone, he refused to even talk to us, saying that customer service wasn't his job.

With that attitude from management, how could you expect anything different from employees? How could you expect to keep customers coming back and wanting to ride the train?

If you were a salesperson—or the president of the company—how would you feel handing over a customer to that kind of organization? You can bring the customers in, you can talk and promise high-level, interdependent relationships, you can promise that the train ride will be spectacular and well worth the time, money, and energy spent. But if the rest of the organization isn't ready, isn't *organized* to keep customers, the customers will no doubt end up feeling as if they have been dumped off the train in hostile territory.

Partnering requires the organization to focus on the customers, not just sales and customer service. In this chapter, we are going to imagine the customer-keeping organization—the organization dedicated to keeping customers and focused on sustaining partnerships.

"Quality is a given. If you can't produce high quality, you might as well not bother, because you won't survive. Exceeding customer expectations is the next battleground." — Wayne Townsend, Saturn

The Worst Game in Town

To begin, think of what is generally regarded as the worst customer game in town: the automobile dealership. This is a story about how that business is being radically changed by the forces of the revolution and by the courage, creativity, and passion of a few revolutionaries.

Saturn: Changing the Game for GM

By now, everyone knows about the multi-billion-dollar GM experiment called Saturn. The Saturn organization was designed around participatory management. The "hard-wiring"—what employees are paid to do—is based largely on a risk-reward formula, in which all share in the profits and the risks. At Saturn, employees are involved in decision making on everything from manufacturing to customer relations. This is unheard-of in the U.S. automotive industry. As a result of such innovative approaches, Saturn products are capturing rave reviews for quality and customer satisfaction.

Pecos River Learning Centers was heavily involved as a training partner in the Saturn start-up. Before the first car was built, all employees at the Springhill plant, including United Auto Workers members, management, and dealer principals, went through a team-building program jointly designed by Pecos River and Saturn.

The Saturn Dealerships: 350 Partnering Organizations

As the Saturn Corporation has reinvented the way cars are made in America, so the Saturn dealerships have "busted the paradigm" of how cars are sold.

Here are some indicators. Rich Perrella, owner of Saturn of Albany, New York, told me not long ago that potential customers come into his facility not because someone said they had to drive a Saturn, but because they were told they had to experience the *sales process* at a Saturn store.

Would you ever tell a friend to go out and experience a car dealership sales process for fun? Why not just tell someone to go to a dentist who doesn't use painkillers?

That got my attention. Clearly, there was something different about the Saturn dealership experience. I next talked to Jim Mayben, sales manager at Saturn of Columbia, South Carolina. He told me that customers have been known to come back to the dealership *to help sell cars.* He also said that, despite all the hoopla of introducing the new car to the public, Saturn dealerships spend an average of only $40 a car on advertising. The industry average is closer to $200 per car. And they can't keep the cars in the stores.

But these are not isolated cases. The widely read and respected 1994 J. D. Powers survey ranked Saturn third in customer satisfaction behind Lexus and Infiniti for the third year in a row. Saturn ranked ahead of the Honda Acura in fourth place and Audi in fifth.

Why get excited about a third-place finisher? With the exception of Saturn, the other four of the top five are all high-priced luxury cars, selling for over $30,000. For the price of any one of those cars, you could buy two Saturns.

So what's going on here?

The story of the Saturn dealerships is an important one, with critical lessons for every company faced with a radically changing environment and changing customers. Saturn has challenged "the way things are" in the business of selling cars by organizing around powerful customer-focused values and tailoring their business operations to meet the needs of customers. Finally, Saturn has provided strong leadership for its sales teams.

Busting Assumptions

The first, and probably most important, thing the Saturn people did was to bust the historical assumptions of the automotive dealership. The initial step in that process was research. They went out and asked consumers what they liked and didn't like about the car-buying experience. Saturn and the dealerships were then organized from the ground up to address the problems identified in the research.

> "From the very beginning, Saturn's goal was to provide a buying and ownership experience that was unparalleled in our car price range. Saturn took a lot of time and effort with customer focus groups to find out, before even making the car, what people liked and disliked about buying an automobile. Then they took those suggestions from customers and tailored the organization around those customer needs."
>
> — Jim Mayben, Saturn of Columbia

As the Saturn dealerships discovered, when an organization tailors itself to the mandates of customers, that choice radically changes the shape and the nature of the company.

Killing the Closers

The biggest gamble the Saturn organization took was to ask customers about the negotiation process—and then act on the answers. Their research revealed that customers hated the financial aspect of the car-buying experience, dealing with "the closer." They said they felt they were up against a professional negotiator and that they had to defeat the negotiator in order to "win."

> "Traditionally, our big problem involved the integrity part of our business, that moment of truth when the customer says, 'Okay, I really like everything, now what is the best price I can get?' For years, we taught our salespeople to start tap dancing at that point because we thought customers would sell us down the river on price. So in two or three minutes of talking about price, we would destroy a couple of hours of relationship building. Saturn changed all this by removing the price issue from the process. It makes our sales process very easy for our salespeople, and it makes it very easy for customers to buy a Saturn."
> — Rich Perrella, Saturn of Albany

Saturn decided to change the game by instituting level pricing: no negotiations, no complicated "pressure selling" around price, and no closers. The sticker price is the price you pay. You also get a special thirty-day, fifteen-hundred-mile guarantee. If you don't like the car, you can bring it back, no questions asked. This went against all of the collective wisdom of automobile dealerships—which ultimately proved not that wise because customers have come in droves to the Saturn alternative.

Most companies look inward for answers and upward for decisions. This "collective wisdom" is the "big brain" theory of organizational management: the big brains are upstairs or in headquarters, far removed from the distractions of customers, away from the grimy and messy business of products and innovation. The big brains make the important decisions in that pure, rarefied atmosphere of the offices with the views, and everyone else, including customers, should leave their brains at the gate and just do what the big brains tell them to do.

This has been how traditional organizations have always made their important decisions about people, markets, and products.

Companies that are serious about keeping customers go at important decisions in a completely opposite fashion. These companies—like Saturn—go to the customer with the important questions, and then act on the information. They allow the customer to shape the company, the products, and the sales and marketing process.

The Nineteenth-Century Organization

Organizing around customers is radical stuff. Think about the traditional organization. It is a military-model, multi-layered hierarchy: bosses, bosses' bosses, managers, vice presidents, directors, and CEOs. One hundred and fifty years ago, it was an amazingly innovative way to organize work and create profit. Now, it's creaking and inefficient. It reminds me of an antique radio with vacuum tubes: old, bulky, and adept only at converting lots of energy into useless heat. But, unlike most old radios, which have long since been replaced by transistorized, computerized models, there are still a lot of old, inefficient, tradition-bound military-model organizations out there acting as if it were still 1970—or 1890, for that matter.

There are all sorts of problems with the military model. It is slow to react and cumbersome to manage. Fear—of losing a job or upsetting a boss—permeates the workplace. Thinking and creativity are discouraged, left to the people upstairs. But the most important problem, from the perspective of keeping customers, lies in how work is organized and for whom work is done.

Whom Do You Work For?

Think of it this way: if you look at the average American company, you discover that most of the employees are amazingly customer focused. They can guess their customer's every whim, they listen to their customer's every idea and wish.

As Dr. Amy Edmondson, a Harvard-trained organizational consultant and Pecos River faculty member, noted in her research, even at the lofty levels of big companies, the customer demands respect. When the customer walks into the room, conversation and arguments cease, heads nod in agreement, and the customer is heard; the old bromide "The customer is always right" springs to life. When the customer says "Jump," even executive vice presidents ask, "How high?"

The problem with most fanatical customer focus is that the "customer" is the company's own management.

In the traditional organization, work is organized around management. Work flows up toward the CEO; employees work for management, not customers. The rewards systems (formal and informal), the reporting systems, the culture, all reinforce . . . what? Pleasing, satisfying, and taking care of the boss.

Inventing the Customer-Keeping Organization

What is being invented today, in the midst of the business revolution, is the company dedicated to the bone to keeping customers. Changing to a customer-keeping organization means busting up the old control-oriented military model and replacing it with a new type of company organized around the customer.

> "To address the issue of partnering, we have had to retool the thinking of the organization. We've had to move away from thinking hierarchy and toward thinking process. In a process, people work together to serve a common objective: the customer. We believe our organization has to be as flat as possible and that people should belong to cross-functional process teams so that they can accomplish the objectives of increasing service levels and customer satisfaction."
>
> — Will Keiper, President and CEO,
> Artisoft Corporation

From the Saturn experience, and from listening to others out there on the edge, we've observed a set of elements that destroy the old assumptions and create an organization focused on partnerships and keeping customers. The customer-keeping organization we "imagine" is based on four principles:

- *Value* the customer
- *Organized* around the customer
- Hardwired to *serve* the customer
- *Leadership*

Value the Customer

> "I think there are subtle mind-sets regarding customers, especially in large, tradition-bound corporations. There is almost a sense of disdain for customers; they can be considered a nuisance. Such organizations tend to assume that customers act out of their worst motives. In some organizations, the prevailing executive attitude is that customers are lucky to have us. This is institutionalized arrogance."
> — Dr. Amy Edmondson

The foundation of the customer-keeping organization begins with the shared belief that the customer is the most important individual in the organization. They are to be appreciated and celebrated. The customer drives the organization, the customer makes it all possible.

From the Heart

This belief is not found in employee manuals or taught in orientation classes. That is to say that every organization teaches that customers are important, the customer is number one. Every fast-food checkout counter in the country no doubt has a sign on the cash register telling employees that the customer is important, that they need to smile and say "Thank-you" to the customer. Valuing the customer transcends training or paying people to be nice to customers. It is a function of beliefs and values.

When we opened up our Pecos River Conference Center in the middle of rural New Mexico, the people we hired from the local areas to work in our dining room and to run the hotel taught me about this kind of service. We were operating on a shoestring and didn't have the money to implement customer service training programs. But we discovered that we didn't have to. The ethic of service, of taking care of important guests, was embedded in that culture, it was from the heart rather than made up in a program. It was common for CEOs and VPs from the East Coast and the Midwest coming through our programs to pull me aside and ask where we found the service people and how we trained them. They were constantly amazed to discover that the caring and the extra touches were what these individuals brought to the job themselves; we had little to do with it.

It is that level of belief, that ethic of service "to important guests," that makes all the difference. From the heart customer focus is the foundation for any organization wanting to be a partnering, customer-keeping company. Valuing the customers and serving the customers have to be seen as the right things to do, not something that you can pay people to do. We should all have a little bit of rural New Mexico in us.

Where do you find these kinds of values and ethics? In the buffalo hunt stories.

"The older I get, the more I believe that the culture of an organization is critical. Culture is the stories we tell about our buffalo hunts. In a sense, a corporation is really a big tribe, very much like the tribes our ancestors belonged to thousands of generations ago. They passed on their culture at night around the fire, when they would talk about what is important, about the hunts and other great experiences. They would talk about all the people who had died and the people who were heroes. All those individuals and all those stories made up the culture.

"That's the same thing we do today. We hear about the heroes and the people who "died." Through the stories, we learn what kind of company we work for—how fair or ethical it is, how it cares for people and customers—all those issues are in the stories. You never hear that stuff in the boardroom; it's in the stories about the hunts.

— Jim DeLong, Miles, Inc., Agriculture Division

"Nobody Cares Like Smith"

Every organization has a cultural mind-set regarding customers.

Smith Furnishings, the innovative retailer in Portland, Oregon, focused on sustaining the culture of caring for customers. The core of their relationships with customers, suppliers, and employees is summed up in their motto, "Nobody cares like Smith."

"Caring about customers is our culture, and it starts from the top down. Most retailers were raised in an adversarial environment, where a good business person was a hard-nosed winner and fought for every last dime. We recognized in the early 1980s that we needed to build a company that was very open and free with information. We took this a step further when we came up with our corporate mission statement, 'Nobody cares like Smith.' We use the term 'partnering' and 'caring' interchangeably because you can't partner unless you sincerely care about the needs and wants of the other person, including suppliers, customers and employees.

"For our customers we've developed a personal guarantee that comes from the value of 'Nobody cares like Smith.' In addition to the factory's and Smith's warranties, our salespeople will give a personal guarantee: if customers have any problems, they can call the salesperson directly. Further, when you buy a product from Smith's, not only will you get a thank-you note, you'll get a telephone call from your salesperson within twenty-four hours after the product has been delivered to make sure you are happy with it and that you understand how it works."

— Glen Grodem, President and CEO,
Smith Furnishings

When caring about customers permeates the organization, a service-oriented culture is created. These are core human values, describing how we all like to be treated and how we like to treat others. What is different is that these companies execute the values, they make them a part of every day's transactions, and those values are the beliefs that underlie the behavior of each worker.

"One of our core beliefs says that we will treat customers the way we treat employees: as members of our family. Compassion has everything to do with our fundamental principles at BB&T, which are trust, responsibility, supportiveness, learning, creativity, and truth. If we interact using these six principles, then we come across as compassionate to our internal and external customers."
— Leslie Spencer, Vice President, BB&T

This might sound like a radical departure from what we were all taught in the business schools, in the trenches, or in the media; but business—and especially business in the future—is ultimately about service to others, no matter where you are in the corporate hierarchy. Forget the idea of subordinates whose sole responsibility is to serve management. Are those folks serving your customers? That's the vital question for the coming decades.

VALUING THE CUSTOMER

✔ *What are the beliefs in your organization regarding customers?*

✔ *What are the "buffalo hunt" stories that are told about customers?*

✔ *What are your beliefs regarding customers? Are they a nuisance, are they adversaries, "problems to be solved"? Or are they collaborators and partners?*

Organized around Customers

"When you start getting concrete about the changes that would have to be made for a company to be organized around the customer, you are talking about areas that are very threatening to people. Partly this is because some people's jobs will be changed or eliminated. Partly it is due to a lack of knowledge of what a customer-centered organization looks like. After years and years of being organized around the product, it's hard even to imagine organizing around the customer."

— Dr. Amy Edmondson

Building on the belief of valuing and serving the customer, the customer-keeping company is organized in whatever manner best supports the mission of keeping customers. When Jim Mayben of Saturn of Columbia talks about having everyone involved with the customer, he means replacing the traditional silos and boxes on the sacred organization chart with a company organized around the customer.

"Customer keeping" drives the structure of the organization, whose future will be cross-functional teams focused on customers, working within flat organizations. In these flatter, faster, and customer-focused companies, everyone understands what drives the business, who the customer is, and how to serve that customer. Position within a company doesn't matter. How high or how deep inside the organization employees work doesn't matter. Whatever the situation, they are linked to, and serve, the customer.

"We've tried from day one to have all our team members become part of the success of the store. There is a spirit throughout the store of wanting to help each other. Communication is better, problem solving goes much easier, and the whole process of running the business is a lot smoother.

"For instance, any salesperson can go straight to a service manager and say, 'Hey, I've got a problem with a customer car.' In a traditional store, salespeople don't talk to the service manager; they talk to the sales manager, who talks to the service manager, creating all kinds of inefficiencies and bureaucratic delays. Working on working together builds enthusiasm, which translates into very high levels of professionalism, ridiculously low staff turnover, and very high levels of customer enthusiasm."
—Rich Perrella, Saturn of Albany

Hardwired to Serve the Customer

Hardwiring is the compensation and rewards system. In order to create the kind of attitudes and behaviors that are at the heart of the customer-keeping organization, the company has to be "hardwired" to support them. The hardwiring needs to support the execution of the mission: serving customers.

All the reinforcement systems need to point the way. Usually, they don't. Usually there is a lot of talk about customers, but very little happens because the rewards and reporting systems stay the same. Pleasing the boss instead of the customer is rewarded, so that's what happens. Companies get what they pay attention to; they get the behavior they reinforce.

"We knew we couldn't support the Saturn idea with a traditional pay plan. So we decided to go to a more innovative way.

"Salespeople have nothing to do with the gross profit on a car sale, since the price is not negotiable. So we put together a pay plan that motivates them to do a complete and enthusiastic sales presentation. We believe that the car sells itself if we tell the Saturn story and how we support customers.

"Our salespeople receive a salary, plus a bonus for every step of the process they take with a customer. They get nothing for selling a car. Out of that process, we get a team approach and a nonpressure atmosphere. Everybody works together and smiles all the time. Customers come in and their comment isn't 'My neighbor bought one of these cars and loves it'; it's 'My neighbor spent two hours telling me how he was treated in the sales process, and I thought I'd better come in and experience it on my own.' Not bad!"—Rich Perrella, Saturn of Albany

HARDWIRING

✔ *What do you pay your employees to do?*

✔ *How does your organization's compensation and rewards conflict with serving customers at an optimal level?*

✔ *How does your hardwiring support serving customers?*

✔ *How can you increase the support and eliminate the conflicts?*

Leadership

> "There is nothing more difficult to take in hand, more perilous to conduct, or more uncertain in its success than to take the lead in the introduction of a new order of things."—Niccolò Machiavelli

Leadership in times like ours is crucial. Leaders are required to point the way, to say, "This is right, this is the way we are going." Leaders, in times of anxiety and ambiguity, are required to cajole, motivate, and help people dream of the future. Business is in large part about people ideas and beliefs. From the beginning, it has taken leaders to create new ideas and challenge old beliefs. It takes leaders to see new possibilities and new ways of working; and it takes leaders to communicate those possibilities to others and move the organization (often kicking and screaming) into the future.

What Is Leadership?

Volumes have been written about leadership, but when you boil it all down, a leader is someone people follow because they want to. Leaders are focused on vision, mission, and, most important, people. Contrary to popular belief, they are not autocrats; they are not in the position to be served, they are there to serve.

This is a critical distinction that has been lost on many a CEO and manager. Just recently, the *Wall Street Journal* carried an article about a *Fortune* 500 company that was experiencing a lot of turmoil and reorganization (what *Fortune* 500 company isn't?). The head of sales and marketing made a presentation to the sales force, saying that he was there to listen and answer questions. He got what he asked for, was asked a tough question, and then went on to "tear the head off" the questioner. According to the article, he continued to belittle the questioner in front of the entire room. That is not leadership. That is the old autocratic game that assumes that only "Caesar" has the answers and everyone else should simply shut up, leave their brains at home and do what Caesar says.

Creating the Vision: Where Are We Going, and Why?

What do true leaders do? First of all, a leader has a compelling vision and mission that are future-focused. Leaders see possibilities, often in large general terms, and are able to motivate others toward that future. The best leaders create an environment where people can focus on things such as innovation and customers. They create an environment where courage and creativity flourish.

Permission, Protection, Tools

In times of great change, leaders often need to provide three critical elements to the people they work with. The first is *permission*: permission to experiment, to try new ways of working, to get outside of the organizational "box," and, finally, to make mistakes during the learning process.

The next element that leadership provides is *protection*.

While change is happening, while people are between trapezes, they need to be protected from the organizational immune system that seeks to kill anything new and different.

Finally, leaders provide *tools*. A tool is anything that helps people do more work with less effort. Tools can help people solve complicated problems and maximize their creativity and productivity. Tools help people create solutions.

The Company's Servant

Ultimately, in today's complicated and rapidly changing business environment, leadership is about serving the people who are closest to the customers, closest to the products, and closest to how the marketplace is really changing. Leaders set direction, but equally important is their task of serving the people who make it all happen, helping to eliminate all the obstacles that get in the way of the people doing the work.

✔ *Leaders create a vision of what is possible and communicate it to others.*

✔ *Leaders guide and support others through their part of the vision.*

✔ *The goal of a leader is to grow and develop people, regardless of the consequences to the leader.*

In our view, leaders are servants, not emperors. Leaders are not aloof, but part of the whole. Leaders do not "tell," they model, they ask questions, they lead by example. Thus leadership is what it should be, a tough, demanding, highly rewarding occupation.

Putting It Together

What do you have when all this comes together? First of all, employees who care deeply about customers. Next, a company organized around customers and employees who are rewarded for adding value to customers. The corporate "hardwiring" makes it easy to serve customers—it's like swimming downstream instead of against the current. Finally, there are leaders pointing the way.

Put it all together and what emerges is a customer-keeping organization.

The New Benchmarks

All over the world, individuals inside companies are asking, "How can we better serve customers?" Almost daily, new and higher benchmarks for customer satisfaction are being established as a means to compete globally. Today's standard will soon be old hat. So where will you be? That's the important question, because it's very easy to get stuck in "the way things are."

Earlier, I wrote that we have yet to see the effects of the full-blown customer revolution. The power and volatility of that revolution are just beginning to make themselves felt. It means new rules and new ways of working together. Responsiveness, speed, and flexibility are the new watchwords.

"My belief is that the life cycle of a business paradigm is diminishing drastically. In the automotive industry, we had a first business model that lasted fifty years. That was the golden era of domestic manufacturing. The next paradigm,

> with skyrocketing fuel costs and foreign competition,
> lasted fifteen years. Now, the business paradigm is chang-
> ing almost yearly." — Wayne Townsend, Saturn

For most organizations, this requires restructuring constantly simply to keep up with customers and technology. As
Glen Grodem of Smith Furnishings says, "We do a little
restructuring every day."

Hard truths, to be sure; but given the scale of change in the
world, it seems inevitable that our companies will also be
transformed. Like sandbars in a riverbed, organizations are
shaped by the rush of the currents around them. Either they
will take the most efficient and effective shape, or they will
be washed away.

Part Three

〰〰〰〰

Incredible Results, More Effective People

The Strategic Abilities of the Future

"What keeps me up at night is worrying about hiring the right people, trusting that they will be able to respond to sophisticated buyers' needs. We can't go on paying people as we have in the past without incredible results. . . . I'm looking for fewer people who are more effective."

—George Brown, Chairman of the Board,
Jardine Insurance Brokers, Inc.

I f we've imagined the future correctly, if partnering is the future relationship between buyer and seller, what is it going to take from salespeople to create and sustain partnerships? What will it take from the individuals working for the customer-keeping organization? And, finally, what will it take from all of us to thrive in this more complex, more competitive "white water"?

What Is It Going to Take?

"We're looking for people who are team players, who have great relationships with customers, and who can drive results."— Lester Knight, Executive Vice President, Baxter Healthcare, Inc.

Strategic Abilities

To be highly effective and to create incredible results in the future will require a new set of beliefs and abilities for everyone in the workplace. The abilities that are required are strategic, they concern how we approach work and what our goals and objectives are. For example, an important strategic ability is being able to drive business results for your customers, to help them make or save money. That is a high-level ability, different from being competent in face-to-face selling.

In this part, we've going to explore the four strategic abilities that will be critical to success in the coming years.

The first strategic ability we call *Playing to Win*. In our permanent white water times, job security is now often a function of being able to make things happen, being able to take the risks to create something new, like new relationships with customers. We also—more than at any time in recent memory—need the emotional muscle to deal with high levels of change and ambiguity, when the answers aren't obvious and the future uncertain.

The ability to create, to take risks, to handle uncertainty is a strategic ability shared by entrepreneurs. The future will require us all to be more entrepreneurial; we each will have to Play to Win—to go as far as we can with all that we've got.

The second strategic ability is *collaboration,* the foundation of teamwork. In a business environment that is more complex and interdependent, everyone in the organization, even those accustomed to doing it by themselves, will now need to be highly skilled in collaboration, in teaming. In this new world order, the operating assumption is "I have to do it myself, but I can't do it alone."

The third strategic ability is *partnership building.* Instead of the "hit and run" business of the past, instead of simply meeting the customer's product and moving on, this strategic ability is focused on always working to improve the relationships, the solutions and the financial benefit to the customer. "Shake it, break it, and remake it" is the operating phrase of this ability.

The last strategic ability we call *driving business results.* The mission at this highest level of partnering is to assist your customers in making money, saving money, or adding value to *their* customers.

Job Description for the Year 2000

Put it all together, and what emerges is a role that is highly entrepreneurial, collaborative, and *important to the customer.* This is the only role for anyone with responsibility for managing customer relationships in the future, the only role for those who want to make a significant impact for their customers and for themselves. It doesn't matter where you live in the organization of the future, these abilities will be crucial to your success.

We're going to explore in detail the strategic abilities vital to success in the coming years. Remember the watchwords, Incredible results and more effective people.

Those are the benchmarks everyone will be measured against. If you can produce incredible results, you will never worry about a job. Employers will beat your door down because they want you. Customers will insist that they work with you. In a far-from-secure business world, this is the most secure of all positions.

Chapter Seven

Playing to Win

 blinding flash of the obvious: The most important ability for anyone "coming to work" today has nothing to do with selling, customers, or business. The most important skill you can bring to work is the ability to thrive in challenging times. As a CEO, whom do I want to hire? People with the courage and creativity to invent the future, who are not threatened by change but actually flourish in it. As a sales manager, whom am I looking for? People who can rise to the challenges being thrown at them by customers, people who can create the new partnering relationships.

Of course, it take skills, knowledge, and experience to work at those levels. But the twin foundations on which everything else depends are courage and creativity. Together, they constitute the ability we call "Playing to Win." Each of us is endowed with this ability, each of us has what it takes to thrive, flourish, and grow in these times. Often, we just need to be reminded of that truth.

How do I know this? Let me explain.

One of the outdoor activities we do at Pecos River is called the Pole. It is a twenty-five-foot telephone pole, with rungs up the side and a round disk on top. Participants are secured into harnesses attached to three safety ropes that are held by their teammates. Each participant climbs up the Pole, stands on top, jumps off, and is lowered to the ground.

It sounds simple. (I know, it also sounds a little bizarre!) But from this simple activity we have learned an enormous amount about the core abilities that we all have and that we need today more than ever.

In 1985, when we started using these outdoor adventure activities in our programs, we didn't know what we were tapping into. I had spent the previous twenty years teaching in traditional classroom settings and being a motivational speaker. I thought I had a pretty good understanding of what motivates people. But we were entirely unprepared for the genie that was unleashed during those outdoor adventure learning days. Over the years, we have tried to understand why activities like the Pole are so powerful, memorable, and even life-changing. Is it simply due to surges of adrenaline or "feel-good" endorphins? Is it peer pressure that makes people do things they would never have considered before?

After years of theorizing, I've come to the conclusion that we are each endowed with courage and creativity. But we lose touch with these abilities because daily life doesn't challenge us to bring forth our courage, passion, and creativity. So, every once in a while, we need a wake-up call to remind us of who we are and what we can accomplish. The Pole, and other activities like it, serve as those wake-up calls.

Here is what we've learned.

When we first explain the Pole to participants, they look at us with disbelief: *You want me to do what?* But after chewing on it for a few minutes, 99 percent of the people we've worked with choose to try—to go as far as they can on the Pole.

Lesson No. 1. *Challenges excite and compel us to try new things, to push ourselves beyond what we think we can do.*

The participants get harnessed up, we do the safety checks, and, one by one, they begin climbing. At some point on the Pole, most people hit a wall of fear that freezes them, even though they are tethered to three safety lines and cannot fall more than six inches.

Lesson No. 2. *Most often the walls of fear, the barriers that we dare not pass, are based not on objective reality, but on subjective, often irrational fear.*

The overwhelming majority of people, after being stuck on the Pole, choose to push through their fear and go higher. Sometimes it's a few inches more, sometimes it's all the way up. How far they go is not important. The fact is that *they have gone farther than they thought they could*, and this becomes a metaphor for them: If I can conquer the fear I had on the Pole, the shaking, the panic, what other fears can I conquer? What real life obstacles can I overcome that previously had me paralyzed with fear?

Lesson No. 3. *We are all capable of doing much more than we believe. We all have more perseverance, creativity under pressure, and courage than we believe we do.*

While all this is going on, the people on the ground, the teammates who may have known the climber only a few hours, are cheering, shouting, and completely focused on supporting the person who is struggling on the Pole. People often remark that the experience of supporting someone else's struggle to conquer the Pole was more powerful and fulfilling than doing it themselves.

Lesson No. 4. *Given the right circumstances, we all seem to be naturally supportive of each other, naturally empathic, and willing to do whatever it takes to help someone who asks for and needs our help. When we come together to support each other, amazing things are possible.*

The Pole is an apt metaphor for the times we find ourselves in: to thrive, change, and grow in times of permanent white water, we must enjoy challenge and be willing to take on risk. This requires overcoming our often irrational fears, those internal voices that tell us to avoid failure and rejection at all costs. We need the confidence to believe that we can do and be more than we think. Finally, we need to know that we can accomplish much more with the support of others than by trying to do it alone.

> "People are amazing. They will respond to the level of responsibility you give them. In adversity, nine times out of ten, if they have good drive and a good spirit, they'll make it all work. Sometimes they've just been waiting for permission to come out of their shells."
> — Jim DeLong, Miles, Inc., Agriculture Division

Such abilities are essential for success and fulfillment in today's world. These are not times for the faint-hearted. These are times for risk takers, adventurers, and entrepreneurs.

Entrepreneur: *A person who organizes and manages an enterprise, especially a business, usually with considerable initiative and risk.*

The common characteristic of entrepreneurs is their perception of themselves as having unlimited personal potential. They typically have great "bounce-back." They make mistakes, occasionally they go down the wrong path, but entrepreneurs are always quickly back in the game. They are accountable for their results, good or bad. Finally, entrepreneurs are willing to take risks.

Psychologists argue over whether risk-tolerance and other "entrepreneurial" traits are genetic, learned, or a combination of both. In any case, wherever we are on the risk-tolerance spectrum, to be fulfilled and successful today, we need to push our personal envelopes as far as possible. We need to risk being uncomfortable, we need to be willing to risk failure to get what we want.

In a Roomful of Drunks in Sioux Falls

Most of us don't attempt to embarrass ourselves purposely in front of family and friends and risk everything we have. Often we bamboozle ourselves into a situation in which we are forced to take some risks and then discover that we can survive and tolerate more than we ever imagined.

I have had many such experiences in the last forty years. One of my first occurred in 1960. At that time, I had a successful insurance business. I was, at thirty, the youngest member of the prestigious Million Dollar Roundtable, and I had five children and a house in suburban Minneapolis. We were content and comfortable. But I was itching to try something new. On a number of occasions, I had been invited to speak to small groups about my success in selling. I enjoyed speaking, but had never considered it as a "career."

All I knew was that I wanted to do something different. And then I heard—this will tell you how naïve I was—that some people actually were paid thousands of dollars for making speeches. This was one of those pieces of information that made the tumblers in the universe click into place for me. People were doing what I loved to do *and* were getting paid for it! I decided that I wanted to be that kind of speaker.

The first thing I did was whip out an envelope and calculate on the back how many speeches I would have to make each month, at what fee, in order to survive financially. Next, I called all my friends to help me find speaking engagements. After three months of "prospecting," I got my first speech, as after-dinner speaker at a sales and marketing convention in Sioux Falls, South Dakota.

I had planned a forty-five-minute speech, with note cards, jokes, and a big motivational ending. I was supposed to go on at 8:00 P.M. The master of ceremonies finally introduced me at 9:00, by which time half the group was drunk and the other half was madly trying to catch up. Well, I lasted ten minutes before the insults and the food began to fly. The people in the front row had their backs to me and the people behind them had either passed out, were engaged in serious food fights, or were yelling at me to get off the stage. From behind the curtain at the side of the stage, I saw the MC motioning wildly for me to get off. Mumbling a final joke, I left the stage—no applause, no thank-yous, the volume in the room simply rose. They had not even noticed me coming or going.

I went back to my hotel room, humiliated, scared, and nearly in tears. What was I going to tell my family? My first feelings were that I had failed miserably. I had sold the insurance agency, I was betting everything I had on making it in this new career, and after months of preparation I had been shot down on day one.

Things looked very grim. But I had made a public commitment to try this new career, so, though sorely tempted, I didn't give up. I made another speech a few weeks later, and then another. Neither was a roaring success, but they helped quell the pain of that first one. I kept learning, I began to enjoy it, and at some point, there was just no turning back.

What made the difference was a combination of determination, a bit of blind optimism on my part, help, and luck. And I learned that you don't die from failure or rejection. I was determined to make it and, once I got my perspective back, I was willing to experience setbacks along the way to success.

After Sioux Falls, I realized that I couldn't do it alone, so I asked for and got help. Bill Gove, one of the truly great business and motivational speakers, was gracious enough to take me under his wing and teach me the business. Finally, luck played a role. I got better, I got speaking dates, and, probably most important, those Sioux Falls sales and marketing executives forgot me and didn't tell anyone about that awful after-dinner speaker at their 1960 convention.

Since then, I've gone through dozens of such experiences, both personal and professional. I have started three companies and was fired—the ultimate rejection!—from the company I founded and that still bears my name. I've been on the edge of bankruptcy more than once, in innumerable situations where a "Yes" or a "No" from a customer determined whether or not my business would survive. Each crisis taught new and invaluable lessons. I've discovered that, with the right perspective and perseverance (and a little luck), we usually end up getting what we want. But fear and anxiety never go away; we just get better at handling them.

These are life strategies shared by most entrepreneurs, by all sorts of adventurers and innovative thinkers. Today, each of us needs to be adventurous, innovative, and entrepreneurial. It is all part of the job description of living in interesting times.

Life Strategies

To help develop our entrepreneurial side and be more risk-tolerant, we first need to examine our current "life strategy." A life strategy is the plan we live by, consciously and unconsciously. It is our map of life, that we've drawn and added to since childhood, based on our parents' teachings and our life experiences. Our life strategy guides our actions and counsels our decisions about risk taking and other serious matters.

In our work, we see two broadly defined life strategies. The first, and most common, is called Playing Not to Lose.

Playing Not to Lose

The goal in Playing Not to Lose is to avoid risk and be comfortable. That all sounds pretty good, right? But we need to look underneath the surface of the strategy to understand what is really going on and what we *truly* risk when we "Play Not to Lose."

> "The Playing Not to Lose epitaph: I survived. I didn't get hurt. I was comfortable. I never lost. I was always right. I never really knew who I was." — Anonymous

Playing Not to Lose is an avoidance strategy, driven by four often unconscious but fatal fears:

1. *Fear of being wrong.* The fear of being wrong can drive us to avoid any situation in which we don't have all the answers. We become so invested in protecting our egos that it is difficult to admit that we don't know everything.

Experienced airline captains have gotten lost, landed short of runways, out of fuel and out of luck, because they refused to admit they could be wrong. They refused to admit that they needed help from a less experienced crew. And many crews have flown to their deaths because they were afraid of telling the captain he was wrong.

A more common, less fatal situation that most of us have experienced is an argument with a loved one, the kind where you knew that you were right. Remember how you felt— furious, determined to win, have the last word, make the other person wrong. Suddenly, in the middle of the argument, you remember something that contradicts your position—maybe you weren't right! But you ignore the contradiction and keep on arguing. Because at that moment it is more important to win the argument, to be right, than it is to discover the truth in a situation.

2. *Fear of failure.* We've grown up being taught that success is everything. Failure is to be shunned at all costs; so we become skilled at avoiding any game in which there is even a remote possibility of failing. When we are afraid of failing, we need to be in control, we pick only the "winnable" battles. Better to play tennis with seven-year-olds (who have never played before) so that we always win. We are never stretched, never pushed to our limits, but we always succeed.

3. *Fear of rejection.* Psychologists tell us that this is the most significant fear of childhood and one that can continue

to control adult lives as adults. When we fear rejection, we do not take risks that could lead to being ostracized. We tend to do what others want us to do rather than what we know is right or what we want to do. We fear being wrong and we fear failure because both lead, ultimately, to being rejected.

4. *Fear of emotional discomfort.* When was the last time you chose not to do something, even though you wanted to, because it would be a little uncomfortable at first? How many things have you not tried, because you might look awkward or foolish? An underlying motivation of Playing Not to Lose is the avoidance of anything that might result in emotional discomfort. The craving to be emotionally comfortable stops us from experiencing new things and from growing. We won't risk looking foolish or stupid. We avoid any situation in which we might be embarrassed, vulnerable, ridiculed, no matter how important it might be for our growth.

We all at some level avoid taking these risks—we play not to lose our "coolness," our professional persona. We attempt to appear to others to be in control, to not let on that we are ever confused or fearful. The classic example of this, the archetype, is the junior high school dance. All those kids desperately want to dance. But no one wants to take the risk of asking someone to dance because they might be rejected, their friends might laugh, they might appear foolish and that would be uncomfortable So you end with boys on one side with their arms crossed, girls on the other side with a few braver girls dancing with each other.

Yet everybody wants to dance.

Everyone wants something out of life, everyone has dreams, ambitions, and abilities. But taking the risk to get what you want often seems impossible, for the same reasons—we might be rejected, scorned, appear foolish, or be uncomfortable. And so we settle for less than we are, even though we really want to dance. We Play Not to Lose.

Playing Not to Lose is the predominant strategy pursued today in our personal lives, in our corporations, in the media and in government. We are inundated with messages telling us to be comfortable, to avoid discomfort, telling us that we can "acquire" happiness and we deserve instant gratification. In our society, it is easy to continue to choose Playing Not to Lose all our lives until we absolutely, positively must face the primal reality: death.

And then it is too late. The ultimate tragedy of Playing Not to Lose isn't that we die. The tragedy is that, arriving at an age where death is a whisper away, we look back on our lives and mourn for the risks we never took, the growth we never experienced, the person we could have been.

✔ *How do you Play Not to Lose in your personal life?*

✔ *How do you Play Not to Lose at work?*

✔ *Why do you Play Not to Lose?*

✔ *Which of the fatal fears is most personal to you?*

✔ *What have you not done in your life—that you wanted to do—because you chose to be comfortable instead or because it would have been inconvenient?*

✔ *What struggle are you in right now?*

✔ *What are you afraid of?*

✔ *What are you going to do about it?*

Thus, the strategy of avoiding, or Playing Not to Lose, is really self-defeating. In the long run, you lose. You lose understanding of who you really are, how tough and resilient you really are, how creative and courageous you can become.

Being a Hero

The alternative strategy is to develop the emotional resiliency and the perspective required to seek and overcome challenges, to tolerate risk, and, when necessary, to endure emotional discomfort. We are all capable of being heroes. Kurt Hahn, one of the most innovative educators of this century and the founder of the prestigious Outward Bound schools, believed this and made it his life's work—to bring out the heroic in individuals.

At the start of World War II, Hahn, already a well-known educator, fled Nazi Germany and landed in England. At the time, British ships were being sunk regularly by German U-boats. Although many of the British sailors made it safely into the lifeboats, large numbers did not survive the ordeal of being at sea in those small boats. They were dying before they were rescued—not necessarily of injuries, but of exposure, and sometimes from just giving up. It wasn't the old salts who were dying, but the young, strong kids of eighteen and nineteen.

The prince of Wales asked Kurt Hahn for his assistance in solving this problem. Hahn's belief was that the younger men did not have sufficient life experience to know that they could endure hardship. Because they didn't believe they could survive, many succumbed and died.

Hahn devised a way to give the young merchant mariners not only the skills required to survive in open boats in the

North Sea, but also the confidence, the perspective, and a taste of the courage required. He did this by having them "go to school" in open boats. They would sail for weeks at a time, to experience and to learn that they had the resources, courage, and the stamina to survive. The program was successful and later became the inspiration for Outward Bound schools all over the world, dedicated to teaching young adults self-reliance, courage, and endurance under difficult conditions—the qualities of the heroic.

By the grace of God, most of us do not have to endure the hardships of those merchant mariners in World War II. Yet there is much we can learn from them. In trying situations, when life reaches down and grabs us, each of us has what it takes to survive and flourish. And that is how life works. We can choose to be or not to be heroes.

Unfortunately, we have perverted the meaning of the word *hero* by using it to describe sports stars and media darlings, as Rev. Jesse Jackson points out, allowing Nike or Reebok to anoint the hero of the moment. But the word hero is a special word, one that is not used lightly in most cultures.

The true meaning of the word hero describes, in every culture, those who are chosen, who are plucked out of their day-to-day existence, who then must endure difficulty and overcome obstacles. As a result of that journey, they are transformed and become more than they were. Heroes rarely volunteer to be heroes. More commonly, they are people like you and me, people who want only to live their lives in peace, but who find themselves in extraordinary situations, where they must call upon their deepest reservoir of courage and creativity. In so doing, they grow; they become larger than they could have imagined, more full of life than they thought possible.

HEROES

Rosa Parks, of Montgomery, Alabama. In 1955, after years of sitting in the back of the bus, she decided to sit up front and thereby helped launch the civil rights movement.

Candy Lightner, who founded MADD, Mothers Against Drunk Drivers, after her thirteen-year-old daughter was killed by a drunk driver. Today, MADD has 320 chapters and 600,000 members nationwide, and is a major force in creating tough DWI laws.

Aung San Suu Kyi, the 1991 winner of the Nobel Peace prize. Suu Kyi was a forty-six-year-old Burmese woman who stood up in vocal opposition to the military junta government in Burma. She was placed under house arrest in 1989, where she has remained ever since.

Terry Fox, the teenage cancer victim. Before he died, he ran three thousand miles across Canada with an artificial leg to raise money for cancer research. His goal was $4 million. His "Marathon of Hope" was so inspirational that individuals and corporations contributed over $30 million.

The lesson is this: all the courage we need to thrive in these times of permanent white water, the creativity we require to invent the future of business and of our lives, we already have. They lie there waiting to be called forth.

If this sounds inspirational, it is meant to be. "Inspired" means the breathing in of the spirit, living by spirit. Nowadays, people tend to be somewhat cynical about such things. Yet, the idea of living an inspired life still resonates for most of us, still calls to us as something *right*.

Playing to Win

We call this spirit, this life strategy, *Playing to Win*. Playing to Win is the alternative strategy to Playing Not to Lose. Playing to Win has nothing to do with the conventional understanding of winning, which is that if I win, someone else has to lose. Playing to Win is a personal strategy defined as *going as far as you can with all that you've got*.

The underlying tenet of Playing to Win is that life is about growing, accepting challenge, and never giving up. The most fulfilled, productive, and loving lives are those in which people have overcome challenges, have grown as a result, and constantly go as far as they can with everything they've got.

Make no mistake, Playing to Win is by far the more difficult strategy, because we often need to endure short-term pain to achieve long-term gain. For example, say you want to start your own business. That usually means you must quit your current job, get a second mortgage on your home, run the risk of failing, and struggle for a few years before it pays off. In the end, if it does pay off, you get to enjoy feelings of fulfillment and success. Yet, most people, when considering the choice, shy away from the commitment, from the risk and the possibility of discomfort.

PLAYING TO WIN

✔ *What do you stand for?*

✔ *What are your life priorities?*

✔ *What inspires you?*

✔ *What are you going to do to get what you want?*

✔ *What are you going to do today?*

Choosing to Play to Win

The key words here are "I choose"—two of the most powerful words in the English language. But as with any powerful incantation, you need to understand them before you use them.

We cannot choose what life will present to us. Life comes at us at out-of-control speed, messy, full on, every second of every day. We can get fifty challenges at work in a day, we get stuck in traffic, we come home to unhappy spouses. Then there are the large life challenges: the birth of our children, the death of our parents, losing a job. Everything can change in a day, everything can change in a second. We cannot predict what life will hand us. It is ultimately out of our control.

But we *can* choose how we want to respond. There is an old saying that God or life never presents us with anything we can't handle—but we have to choose to handle it. Every moment of our life is a choice, and each choice has consequences.

> "In nature there are neither rewards nor punishments—there are consequences." — Robert Ingersoll

Choosing, Risking, and Learning

The Playing to Win strategy is this: to consciously and rationally make the choice to go as far as we can with all that we've got, as often as we can. Frequently, this involves choosing growth over comfort. It often involves taking risks.

Dick Leider, author of *The Power of Purpose*, brings an important perspective to this question. He interviewed a number of people in their eighties and nineties, asking, "If you could live your life over again, what would you do differently?" Two major themes emerged from all the responses. First, people said that if they could do it over, they would take more risks, both emotional and physical. They don't have to be big risks, like scaling mountains; they can be small at first, as we tackle the small dragons of our lives. As we grow stronger, we can take on larger dragons. But what allows us to take *intelligent* risks is the second part of the seniors' answer: taking more time to reflect, to understand, to learn from experiences.

Taking the time to learn from our experiences makes all the difference. We need to slow down on occasion and listen to our fears—are they rational, or irrational? Asking ourselves: Are we doing what we truly want to do and do we have choice? (We usually do.) Everything we learn can be applied to the next challenge in our lives. Every time we overcome a fear, an obstacle, we become more heroic, larger and wiser than we were. Risking and learning are the models for growing as a human being, growing this internal capacity called Playing to Win.

Courage, Creativity, and Reason

"Courage is the price that life exacts for granting peace. The soul that knows it not knows no release from little things."— Amelia Earhart, aviator

The key that unlocks all this potential is the great gift we've been given, this underappreciated, underutilized gift: the ability to reason. I remember the speech that Barbara Jordan, former congresswoman from Texas, made at the 1992 Democratic Convention. She concluded by quoting William Allen White, the late editor of the Emporia, Kansas, *Gazette*, who wrote: "Reason never has failed men. Only fear and oppression have made the wrecks in the world."

Barbara Jordan spoke about reason in the context of politics and society, but the same principle applies to us as individuals. Reason and rational thinking will rarely fail us as we face our own daily battles. Reason is our chief weapon against those personal dragons of insecurity and doubt. It is our chief ally in the quest to go as far as we can with all that we've got.

When we use reason, courage, and creativity, we get to live life fully, we get to be among those who are constantly challenged, constantly growing, and always alive. That is what's important; that is how we can make a difference for ourselves and truly Play to Win.

"I'd dare to make more mistakes next time. I would limber up. I would take fewer things seriously. I would take more chances. I would climb more mountains . . . I would perhaps have more troubles, but I would have fewer imaginary ones.

"You see, I am one of those people who live seriously, day after day. I've been one of those people who never goes anywhere without a thermometer, a hot water bottle, a raincoat, and a parachute. If I had it to do over again, I'd travel lighter than I have. I would start barefoot earlier in the spring and stay that way later in the fall. I would go to more dances, I would ride more merry-go-rounds. I would pick more daisies."— Nadine Stair, at age eighty-six

Chapter Eight

~~~~~~~~~~

"I Have to Do It Myself, but I Can't Do It Alone"

I had a glimpse of the future of relationship selling a few years ago, during a meeting with a large customer we had been doing business with for years. Our two companies had finally jointly decided that it was time to launch a partnership.

The first thing I noticed when I walked into the meeting room was that at least twenty people were gathered around the table. Our customer's senior vice president was there, along with the other contacts in the organization. But there were also individuals I didn't recognize. In addition, there were people from our company who had never been in front of a customer before—design people, accounting people, even our office manager.

What I understood at that moment was, first, how complex business relationships had become. Until now, business, especially selling, was normally conducted in one-to-one relationships. In the future, partnership builders (whether they are salespeople or senior management) will require skill in facilitating, coaching, leading, and mentoring teams of people. To be a master at creating partnerships, one needs to be an expert at bringing together people from all over the organization, with all sorts of opinions, ideas, and motivations, to create teams. Cross-functional, cross-organizational

159

teams are at the core of partnering relationships between organizations.

Teams are how we will get important work done in the future. Teams are where the relationships will be created, where problem solving will take place. Teams are where partnerships will be truly forged.

Terry Mulligan, the vice president of corporate sales for Baxter Healthcare, the $8 billion hospital and medical equipment supplier, goes so far as to say that the most vital skill in the future for everyone in the workplace will be the ability to work on teams. This has major implications for all of us.

The future of doing business with important customers will require that we discard the old model of the Lone Ranger salesperson and replace it with a diverse, committed group of people working closely together to serve and keep customers. Some of those people will be salespeople, some will be product specialists, some executives. They will be united by the overriding mission of working together to meet the needs of customers.

Customers, now and in the future, are too important and too demanding, and their issues too complex, for one salesperson to handle. The underlying truth is that individuals working by themselves—no matter how intelligent and experienced they might be—simply do not have the answers or the breadth of knowledge to respond appropriately to this environment. That is a broad generalization, but it is becoming a reality for more and more industries.

"To me, it is folly to think that one sales rep and one buyer can represent the total complex system. No individual is equipped to do that, no matter what kind of superstar

> he or she might be. One of the first things we have to do is change from a one-to-one system to a multifunctional high-performance selling team approach. When you put those teams together with a customer's multifunctional team, miracles can happen.''
> — Lou Pritchett, former Vice President, Sales, Procter & Gamble

Customer issues are often of a higher order of complexity than ever before. Instead of product solutions, for example, customers want system cost reduction and service implementation, things that are often ``outside of the box'' of the traditional individual sales rep.

The cycle of business has become faster. Customers and salespeople can't wait for requests and problems to go up the old military-model chain of command. They need solutions now.

Customer relationships and customer information are too valuable to be the sole property of one salesperson. Too often, customer information is not spread through the organization, not understood, and not even ``stored'' in a manner that the organization can access. When a salesperson leaves the organization (or is sick, or on vacation), poof! so does the information, and often so does the customer.

From Solo to Collaboration

Teams of people will work with the customer in the future. Teams that are empowered to make decisions, that share information and bring a larger array of expertise to the customer than an individual salesperson.

Yet moving to a collaboration will require a basic change in work and working relationships. As companies like Baxter Healthcare have discovered, people don't automatically begin cooperating instead of acting on their own. It rarely happens by executive order or because it is just the right thing to do.

Teamwork has to be learned, or, from the perspective of Plato, relearned.

Team Genes

Plato wrote that most learning is rediscovering what we already know. Much of what we are "learning" today, about ourselves and about working together, we already know at an intuitive level. The history of humanity suggests that the team—a group of people working and living together to serve a higher purpose (called survival)—is among the most primal and basic instincts of being human.

One of my favorite books, one that changed the way I think about "us," is William Calvin's *The River That Flows Upstream*. Calvin is a neurobiologist and his book is a collection of musings and conversations with a group of scientists as they raft down the Grand Canyon, dealing primarily with who we are and where we came from. Calvin writes,

Evolution shaped us from pre-humans to humans over at least 100,000 generations; the 400 or fewer generations that we've spent away from the hunting and gathering life style probably hasn't changed our gene pool very much. Our deep roots are to ice-age tribes; although we seem extraordinarily flexible and adaptable, our civilized behaviors are inevitably an overlay, a frosting.

In other words, for most of our existence as a species, human beings were born into, lived and worked with, fought for and died in, small communities—in tribes, or hunting and gathering groups. From the Ice Age until quite recently, a highly valued competency was the ability to adapt to that small community environment, which required high levels of cooperation, communication, loyalty, and trust. Those abilities were passed down as survival skills through 100,000 generations. The consequence of not being part of a collective, a tribe, or a team was death. The Ice Age world was too dangerous and complex for individuals to survive on their own.

Contrary to what we have been taught, and contrary to our current cultural myths, the fact is that we are born to collaborate, to work together. The problems we face have changed, but that innate talent for working to achieve a common goal hasn't. We are collaborators. We work best when we work together. The rugged individual out there conquering the frontier (like the Lone Ranger) is mostly a myth. The vast majority of us are natural team players; it's in our genes, in our bones, part of our collective inheritance. It is how we are wired up.

So Plato was right. In the workplace, faced with a more complex and "dangerous" environment, where the consequence of not being as creative and productive as possible is corporate "death," we are coming together, rediscovering something we already knew: collaboration and cooperation are the best way to survive and thrive.

And, yet, for the average American salesperson or anyone else who is part of the corporation, learning to work in teams doesn't happen automatically. The reason is obvious. On the collaboration/competition spectrum, our culture is way over on the competitive end. We have learned and practiced competition in this country for so long that we believe, at some level, that it is the way things are. As Marshall McLuhan said, "We don't know who it was that discovered water, but we are pretty sure it wasn't fish"—the point being that the more powerful the cultural norm, the less likely we are to even be aware of it. For us, competitiveness is a powerful cultural norm. We swim in the seas of competitiveness, unaware that there are other options.

We see the results of this "cultural training" all the time in our programs. For example, simply divide a group of people into teams and they automatically behave as if they are competing with one another. The two teams, even if they are working on similar tasks, rarely consider asking each other for help, or even observing each other's solutions. (We were all taught in school *that* would be cheating!!!) That's how deeply ingrained the idea of competing is.

For those of you who are thinking, "Competition is the American way—it's how we built this country!" I would politely suggest that you are wrong. This country owes much to collaboration, to working together to solve complex problems. Competition is only one of a myriad of possible roads to solving problems or motivating people. If we believe it is the *only* road, we miss the other possibilities. We all have competition out there in the real world, companies that are going after our market share, our profitability. We need to focus our competitive spirit on those threats. At the same time, faced with more complex problems, more demanding customers, we need to build collaboration and cooperation internally.

What Is a Team?

To answer this question, I thought it would be important to listen to an organization that is devoting serious time and energy to creating teamwork in its sales force: Baxter Health-care, Inc. Baxter is in the midst of reorganizing its national sales force into teams focused on its hospital and industrial customers. One of the individuals responsible for ground-breaking research on teams is Frank Lafasto, Baxter's vice president for human resources and development. Frank has been involved with over one thousand teams in the last two decades. His work has been instrumental in helping Baxter understand and implement teams in its national sales force.

Frank defines teamwork as a collective effort toward a common goal. A team can be two people or it can be thirty people. It can be made up only of salespeople, or it can be a highly cross-functional mix. What unites a team isn't the job descriptions, but the unity of purpose, the common goal.

What Do Teams Do?

What do teams do that is different from the same group of people working individually? As we see it, teams are responsible for five functions.

The first three categories have to do with the shared task of the team. For example, a production team is required to produce a certain amount of ''stuff'' every day. A sales team has quotas and needs to drive results. These tasks are the *work* that the team shares in common. When the work begins to break down, or when there are glitches or problems, the team moves to its next level of competency: it *problem solves*. Problem solving can mean anything from

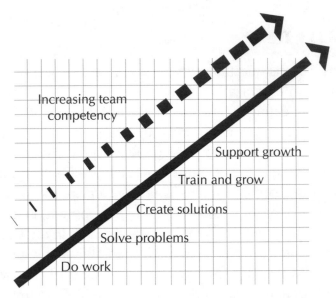

"Hey, we got a problem" to using total quality management processes to solve more complex problems. Teams might bring in help and ask for advice, but they "own" the problem until it is resolved.

When confronted with a problem in which the solution is not simply a matter of a small change, teams *create* new solutions.

> "From a customer's point of view, Baxter has sometimes been complicated to deal with. For example, customers get multiple invoices from Baxter's different divisions. This can be a major headache for the customer. One of our teams decided, on its own, to solve this problem. The team worked on the problem and in a few weeks put together a system that produced a single amalgamated invoice for each customer—something that Baxter had never been able to do before."— Joe Sfara, Corporate Sales, Baxter Healthcare, Inc.

The last two tasks of a high-performing team have to do with team development and learning. On high-performing teams, the team is responsible for the *professional and personal growth* of the team and its members. The team is the forum for training, feedback, and growth. The team trains new members and evaluates and sets standards of performance and behavior for all members.

Finally, the team functions as a *support* group for its members in their work and growth. The team is the place to go for help, ideas, and support.

A fully functioning, high-performing team moves easily between all of the tasks and shifts gears smoothly. Each competency requires different skills and different leadership. Healthy teams move leadership around to those individuals most competent for the task at hand. On a team, it's not about stripes on your shoulder, it's about who can best do the job.

Excellent teams evolve to a level where they are self-managed, fairly autonomous, and highly productive. They work hard and they work well together. But it doesn't happen by accident. Underlying the ''best of the best'' teams are some shared traits that make a difference.

Characteristics of High-Performing Teams

Our experience with thousands of workplace teams at Pecos River Learning Centers strongly reinforces Baxter's conclusion that there are three ''broad-brush'' characteristics critical to high-performing, energized teams:

1. A clear and elevating goal.

2. A trusting and supportive environment.

3. High standards and shared accountability.

A Clear and Elevating Goal

People need to do significant things. We are at our best when we are engaged in important tasks. John Allison, the president of BB&T, the innovative and highly successful North Carolina bank, puts it this way: "If you are not doing something important, you have to change what you are doing, because people are here to do important work."

Team Zebra's Dramatic Improvement

You learn from your customers. Kodak's black-and-white film division is a testament to the power of reengineering, teams, and doing important work.

Kodak had a problem with cycle time—the time it took to move from customer order to delivery. Fuji, one of its competitors, had a cycle time less than half that of Kodak. To stay competitive, Kodak needed to reduce a forty-one-day cycle in its black-and-white film division.

Analysis of the problem revealed that there were at least five departments involved in the cycle. Their traditional relationship was the old "over the wall" strategy: research has an idea and throws it over the wall to manufacturing, who manufactures it and throws it over the wall to sales, and so on. There was very little communication between departments.

In response to this important problem, Kodak organized a cross-functional team from the five departments and sent the members through a Pecos River Changing the Game program to help them pull together quickly as a team, understand the problem, and "kick start" the process. This self-titled "Team Zebra" determined that the problem was caused not by technological constraints, but by delays between different organizational functions, each responsible for different steps in the value chain.

Team Zebra took on the challenge of whittling away at that "normal" forty-one-day cycle. Their "clear and elevating" goal was to get it down to five days—an ambitious target and one that they were unable to accomplish in their first attempt. They did achieve a game-changing thirteen days, a significant decrease from forty-one days. Team Zebra was able to do this by changing the way that the five different areas involved in the sequence worked together. This successful reduction of over 68 percent on the cycle time represented enormous financial returns for Kodak.

As is typical with high-performing teams, Team Zebra was not satisfied. They set a new cycle time goal—of *one day!* They did not actually expect to achieve a one-day cycle time; they just wanted to see what they could learn from trying. Part of what they realized from their successful effort of reducing the cycle from forty-one to thirteen days was *how much they learned* about the process that no one person really had grasped before.

The keys? They were galvanized by an important problem, defined in this case by a hugely competitive challenge. Important problems energize people, get their juices flowing. Next, there was a clear goal: to reduce cycle time as much as possible. The goal was not just to "beat Fuji," but to continually reduce cycle time to its mathematically ultimate limit. That, incidentally, is the difference between "playing to win" and merely choosing a goal. When a team goes as far as it can, goals are secondary. Continuous improvement is what is important.

The final key was a cross-functional team: constructed of individuals who had a stake in the outcome. They were all deeply involved and had "permission" to attack the problem, "protection" from management to seek nontraditional solutions, and "process" tools to do the work.

The learning: *Teams work best when the mission is important, the goal clear, and the stakes high.*

Trust Is the Foundation

Trust: *Reliance on the integrity, strength, ability, surety, etc., of a person or thing; confidence.*

A clear and elevating goal gives teams direction and makes them successful against tasks. The foundation upon which all of that is built is trust. High-performing teams have high levels of trust.

> "Trust comes inch by inch. And there are some critical events that helped it happen. When you see a rep give up something for someone else, making a sacrifice for a teammate, that begins to change things. It's not just the two people, the one sacrificing and the one receiving; it's everyone else watching and thinking, 'Whoa, this is serious. It means something.' That's when trust takes off and you can start to see and feel the difference."
> — Joe Sfara, Corporate Sales,
> Baxter Healthcare, Inc.

For a team, trust is like healthy and fertile soil. Plants flourish when all the nutrients are in the soil. When the soil is barren, or out of balance, nothing can grow. So it is with teams. The "soil" has to be rich and fertile, full of trust, in order for teams to flourish.

T=A.S.T.E.

We spend a lot of time helping teams understand and practice the healthy dynamics of teams and trust. We then give them the tools to use back in the workplace to "continually improve" their team skills. We teach that the foundation of trust is built upon four elements:

1. *Accountability.* Individuals and the team take accountability for their actions, decisions, mistakes, and successes.

2. *Support.* Team members support each other around the tough issues, like telling the truth and taking risks.

3. *Truth.* Team members are committed to and support each other in telling the truth as each team member sees it. This applies especially to the unpopular truth.

4. *Energy.* Team members are willing to commit time and energy to the team. They are willing to go as far as they can, with all the energy they have, to help the team grow and be successful.

High Standards and Accountability

The final characteristic of a high-performing team is that it sets high standards and takes accountability for those standards. When people have important work to do, they embrace high standards. The supportive, trusting environment of a true team encourages individuals to set standards and be accountable, because they know that they are not alone and that it's okay to take risks and make mistakes in pursuit of the goal.

Put simply, teams bring out the best in individuals. For example, participants in our outdoor programs come up against physical challenges that initially seem impossible. Yet, when the team begins working together to solve the problem and create solutions, the impossible becomes merely difficult. Light bulbs go on. As the day progresses, everyone realizes that the team can accomplish much more than they had ever thought possible. They raise the bar of their performance standards. When they move into the classroom to tackle real-world problems, the standards for accomplishment stay intact.

Teams turn up the heat on all of us to perform at our best. We don't want to let our teammates down. The support from a healthy team removes the fear of looking foolish or making mistakes, so we are willing to take more risks. Finally, high performance is being modeled for us by our teammates. It's infectious.

The learning: *If you want high-performing individuals, put them in high-performing supportive team environments.*

When teams set their own standards and objectives, they tend to hold themselves accountable to those standards. For example, according to Baxter's Joe Sfara, one cross-divisional sales team for Baxter set the objective that every divisional salesperson represented by the team would finish this particular year in the black. Toward the end of the year, a few of the divisions were in the red. At that point, in order to meet the goal of everyone's having a successful year, the entire team stopped what they were doing and focused on getting business for those divisions.

Team Building

It is a waste of time and energy to create teams unless there is a clear and compelling reason to exist. Teams do important work and shouldn't be formed for anything less. Then they need a supportive and trusting environment based on "TASTE": Trust = Accountability, Support, Truth, and Energy. Finally, expectations for performance need to be high, engaging, and challenging.

Collaborating, "teaming" at this level, means giving up some of the traditional ways we've been rewarded; it means sharing customers, information, and eventually compensation. But teams give us the opportunity to leverage our knowledge and our relationships in a much more productive manner. Teams are about working smart—getting more for less effort by working together. And that feels good. We are at our best when we are together. That hits pretty close to what we all want: to be in an environment where we can do our best.

Beyond Teams: Boundarylessness

The word "boundarylessness" was coined by Jack Welch, CEO of General Electric. It captured my imagination as a descriptor of what exists beyond teams: collaborations that stretch past a company's boundaries to embrace suppliers and customers. The work of tearing down the boundaries is happening today in hundreds of new kinds of relationships created by salespeople, by customers, and by organizations.

The inclusion of customers on your teams is an essential part of this boundaryless future. Baxter Healthcare has one such boundaryless team working with Boston University Hospital. That team, which meets weekly at the hospital, also includes the hospital's customers. The team leader is purchasing manager Nancy Hallgren.

> "Over the past five years, we've seen the relationship move from adversarial to win-win. In the past, suppliers would try to sell something at the highest possible price, and we would try to get the lowest possible price. Now Baxter and our hospital staff are working closely together to solve a whole range of problems that we have. The meetings are casual, off the cuff, and focused on solving problems and developing solutions.
>
> "For example, we had a problem in our pharmacy when the hospital replaced the hall carpeting with tiles without telling anyone. The Baxter carts we were using at the time to deliver solutions promptly tore up the tiles. It wasn't anyone's fault, but we had to solve the problem. We took it to the Baxter meeting and worked together on the solution. The Baxter team, out of their own pockets, bought new carts because they wanted to solve the problem.
>
> "In the past, it would have been our problem and we would have had to figure it out. Now we can work it out together with more ideas and more resources. That's the difference a team can make."
>
> — Nancy Hallgren, Boston University Hospital

What We Have In Common

When you begin to take down the barriers that we've all had a part in constructing (I work for this division, you work in that department, and she is the customer), we discover that we have much in common, that it feels good to work together, to cooperate rather than compete. Together, we perform at higher levels. We are more creative, more supportive, and more willing to take risks.

If I were to hire for the "future perfect" organization geared to thrive at the turn of the century, I would search for different kinds of people than in years gone by. Instead of "Lone Rangers," I would seek collaborators. Instead of those who play it safe, and always say yes to the boss, I would seek out risk takers. I would seek those who set high expectations for themselves and those around them. Then I would put them on teams, and help them create a supportive and accountable environment—and then I would get out of the way. Those teams could take on the world.

The future of business belongs to people who collaborate, who seek out cooperative solutions and situations, who are natural team members and leaders. That is a fairly dramatic shift from the way things used to be. But the world has changed. It has become smaller, faster, and more complex. We can no longer accomplish everything by ourselves. There is much for the individual to do, but doing it with a team is the way of the future for most of us.

Which brings us back to the Pole: "Given the right circumstances, we all seem to be naturally supportive of each other, naturally empathic, and willing to do whatever it takes to help someone who asks for and needs our help. When we come together to collaborate, to support and take care of each other, amazing things are possible."

In the future, our jobs will be to create these circumstances, to create an environment where people come together. When you bring a team of people together, give them important work, provide an atmosphere of trust and accountability. They will amaze you with the work they do, and with their power and creativity.

We are all capable of amazing things. Equally important, we are all capable of bringing out amazing things in other people, when we care for them, when we support them, when we are on their team.

The last question I asked Nancy Hallgren was this: "If you could tell all the salespeople that you deal with one thing, what would it be?" Her answer sums it up. She said: "Don't be afraid to cooperate and collaborate with your customers or with people in your own company. The reality is that we depend on each other. If we don't work together, none of us is going to make it."

Spoken like a true partnership player.

Chapter Nine

~~~~~~~~~

Growing Partnerships

I t was 5:00 P.M. in a crowded London grocery store. All checkout lines were backed up and customers and grocery carts packed the store. The clerks were checking customers and their groceries with that high-speed, single-minded rhythm when, without warning, every computerized register in the store went blank. The scanners quit, the computer screens went dark. A collective groan was heard throughout the store. The clerks looked at each other—there was no manager in the store to tell them what to do. They quickly huddled together to figure out a solution. Then they came back to their registers and made an announcement. They would gladly continue to pack groceries if the customers would simply pay what each customer estimated they owed. And so, for the next few hours, the lines moved, the customers paid their estimates, and at the end of the day, the customers all had their groceries and the store was financially ahead.

Think for a moment of the pressures the clerks were under when they huddled together. It would have been easy to Play Not to Lose, get out the hand calculators and do it by the book. That would have made the customers miserable and angry, but the accountants would've been happy. But the clerks devised a solution (for a problem that wasn't in the operating manual) that would please the customer first. As a result of their quick thinking and customer focus, the store made money and more importantly created, no doubt, a few customers for life.

The clerks were able to develop the solution because they had the customers' best interests at heart. The priority was to help their customers get what they wanted. Next, they developed a creative, "out of the box" solution that met the needs of the customers and the store.

Positive Intention and Creativity

The actions of those London grocery clerks exactly describe the ability required to grow and sustain long-term relationships. It takes positive intention and creativity focused every day, from everyone in the organization, to keep a partnership growing and alive.

Results and Relationships

Partnerships require—from the customer perspective— bottom-line economic benefit. It drives the partnership. But running a close second, the relationship needs also to be positive and growing. In this chapter, we are going to explore the relationship side of partnerships; how to grow long-term relationships with positive intention and creativity.

Growing, Growing, Growing

Growing partnerships is a strategic ability that everyone involved in a business needs to understand. The newest hire to the CEO are part of growing and sustaining partnerships. The definition of growth explains why this is so. Growth is defined as making increasingly more complex connections. Organisms start out as single cells and grow into more complex and interconnected multicellular animals. Children emotionally and intellectually grow by making increasingly complex connections with the people and environment around them.

A relationship with a customer often starts out with a single relationship between a salesperson and a buyer. The relationship grows when the connections multiply. Besides the salesperson and buyer, there are connections between executives, between accounting functions, between shipping and receiving. As the relationship continues to grow, more connections are made between the organizations.

Imagine the powerful partnership that would be created if every one of those connecting points was driven by that London grocery store's positive intention and creativity. Imagine the power of the relationship if everyone involved asked daily: "How can I help 'grow' this relationship?" "What can I do daily to create customer-pleasing solutions?"

Growing partnerships requires everyone to participate, to be connected to the customer or to at least be aware that there is a partner, a customer, out there that requires special treatment.

When the college-age kid, working the part-time graveyard shift, understands that there is a partner out there, then the organization is headed in the right direction, committed to growing partnerships.

Going, Gone, Dead

A compelling reason for this level of commitment—a reason many salespeople stay up half the night gulping antacids—is what happens when their company is not committed to customers, when people in the company aren't even aware that there is a customer out there. In those situations, the customer calls and is treated with apathy, ignorance, or, worse, rudeness. The customer calls and is instantly assaulted with policies and procedures that make it difficult to do business. All of this is out of the salesperson's control, which is why it is so difficult for him or her to "let go" of a customer to the organization. In so many circumstances, salespeople don't trust that the organization values customers with the same intensity that they do. They live and die with customers. Obviously, so does the company, but often companies don't act like it.

Partnering will not survive those kinds of companies. A partnership will die before it is born if there is no relationship strategy, if the entire organization is not vibrating with enthusiasm and support for the partnership.

In a survey done by *U.S. News and World Report,* they asked the question, Why do customers leave a business? Here is what they heard:

■ The business moved	9%
■ Didn't like product	12%
■ Price increase	11%
■ Treated rudely by employee	69%

It is not enough to eliminate rudeness. Partnerships require the proactive spirit and customer focus of the London grocery store clerks. At every connecting point of the partnership, the focus has to be there: What does our partner want and how can we create solutions?

What Do Partners Want?

Customers basically want three things: an adequate solution (a solution that solves the problem, not to be confused with an inferior solution), a trusting relationship, and value-added service. A partner, of course, wants and expects the same thing, except that it is not just one or two transactions, but over the life of the partnership—and that is what creates the problem and the opportunity.

The problem is that long-term relationships are dynamic—they are either getting stronger or weaker, they rarely stay the same. If we do nothing to improve and grow the relationship (at all those connecting points), it will grow weaker and ultimately crash.

> "Routine maintenance is our only defense against a universe spinning out of control."—*Hill Street Blues*

The routine maintenance of partnership building involves a belief, a mind-set, and three strategies. Think of these as a partnering checklist. They are "what to do" on a routine basis to grow a partnering relationship.

1. The wonderful paradox

2. Break it, shake it, and remake it

3. Manage the moments of truth

4. Value-added service

5. Run toward problems

1. The Wonderful Paradox

Positive intention toward customers comes from the heart. Having your customer's best interests at heart is like breathing. It is a fundamental business ethic, springing from a deep belief of what is right. If it doesn't feel right for you to put the customer first, if you cannot trust the customer or serve the customer, then you do not belong in the free market. Seek work in government.

Having your customers' best interests at heart is also the foundation of growing partnerships. Simply put, it means that when a problem comes up, or there is an issue that needs to be decided, the first point of view is "What is in the best interest of the customer?"

Although this sounds altruistic, even naïve, it actually is in the best interests of you and your organization to believe, think, and behave with your customer's best interests at heart. First, it's the right thing to do, and the free marketplace has its own natural laws that govern how the business universe works. A principal law of that universe is the wonderful paradox: I get what I want by helping others get what they want.

Everything we want for our business, everything we want in our careers, for supporting our families in our economy comes as a result of serving customers. This is a powerful point of view because it focuses all our energy and creativity right where it needs to be: on the customer.

Every morning, the question is, How can I take care of our customers today? Every time there is a problem or glitch, What is in the best interests of my customer?

When everyone in the company—at all those "connection

points"—holds that belief, when everyone is living the wonderful paradox, then the maximum amount of energy, creativity, and enthusiasm will be focused where it need to be—on growing the partnership.

2. Break It, Shake It, and Remake It: The Mindset of Partnering

Everybody knows at least one tinkerer. He or she is the person who is never satisfied with something they've created or fixed. They are constantly fixing it, improving, tearing it apart, and starting over. They often drive the rest of us crazy, because whatever they're working on is never finished. My in-law, Ward Edwards, owns one of the oldest wooden sailboats in the state of Minnesota. He has owned it since he was a kid. He is constantly working on it, fixing, sanding, varnishing, and replacing parts. It is more than just a boat, it is an obsession, it is art and passion combined. It is also impeccable.

That mentality—fixing, improving, never being satisfied—is one of the competitive advantages of the Japanese called kaizen, or continuous improvement. This is so deeply ingrained in Japanese culture that they are barely aware of it, it is just what is so. There is never a fixed goal, for example, a production model of a car that was fixed in stone. Instead, it is a constant process of improvement, fixing and . . . tinkering. The mind-set of continuous improvement is to learn from each experience and change, based on what you have learned, and repeat the process.

This is the same mind-set that can be applied to the partnering relationship. Again, it is a mind-set that everyone facing the customer should hold.

✔ *How can we improve our service?*

✔ *What can we do better?*

✔ *How can we respond faster to customer requests?*

✔ *Can we change our invoicing to make it easier for the customer?*

✔ *How can we be easier to deal with?*

✔ *Can we be less expensive?*

✔ *How can we drive out unnecessary costs?*

✔ *What have we learned?*

✔ *What can we change and improve?*

If positive intention is the heart of building partnerships, then continuous improvement is the way to think, the mind-set of partnering. The challenges and question behind continuous improvement go on forever. There is always "positive dissatisfaction," always the need to do it better. The creative person is always breaking, shaking, and re-making. The sailboat is constantly being rebuilt.

3. Manage the Moments of Truth

There is that moment, by way of example, sitting in the office of a car dealership, having just signed the contract. Expectations run high. In that moment, everyone professes quality, service, and impeccable values.

But the truth lies in the details after the car is driven away. What happens when the customer calls to make a service appointment? How long does the phone ring before it is picked up? Is the caller transferred to the right department?

Is the service person friendly, helpful, or annoyed by the intrusion? Is the problem fixed the first time? Is the bill right? And so it goes. A long-term relationship, whether it is with a car dealership or in a partnership with a customer is made or broken in the details, in those moments that often only the customer knows about.

Scandinavian Airlines CEO Jan Carlzon understood that airlines are the ultimate low switching cost commodity businesses (like the film that Kodak and Fuji make, the boxes might be different colors, but the insides are all the same). Carlzon believed that competitive advantage lay in things other than airplanes, routes, and fares. In his book *Moments of Truth*, he wrote: "Last year each of our ten million customers came in contact with approximately five SAS employees, and each contact lasted an average of fifteen seconds. Thus, SAS is created fifty million times a year, fifteen seconds at a time. These fifty million moments of truth are the moments that ultimately determine whether SAS will succeed or fail as a company."

Every interaction between your customer and your organization is a moment of truth. Face-to-face meetings, telephone calls, correspondence, when a customer arrives at your facility, when a customer receives your product, how problems are dealt with, and when the customer receives an invoice—all these are moments of truth.

The Anatomy of the Moment

Each one of these moments of truth is an opportunity to meet or exceed your customers' expectations. They have expectations of how things *should* work or how they *should* be treated. And these are *their* expectations, not ours.

For example, let's analyze a simple moment of truth. A buyer calls the office to find out about a billing error:

Moment of Truth	Buyer Expectation
Places the call to your office.	Phone is picked up by third ring.
Receptionist answers.	Clear and friendly response.
Asks for information.	Handled appropriately, transferred to the correct person.
Call is transferred.	Phone is picked up by third ring.
Accounting answers.	Clear and friendly response.
Problem stated.	Problem handled appropriately in a friendly and timely manner.

Buyers have expectations each time they interact with us. How we respond to those expectations determines whether they are satisfied, unhappy, ecstatic, or angry. And that affects whether they stay or leave.

Understanding Expectations

The objective is to understand, and then continuously improve, the moments of truth. First, decide which moments of truth are critical to the customer. The next step is to ask customers to identify their expectations at each one of those important moments of truth.

This can be subtle stuff sometimes. For example, we had a customer who was clearly dissatisfied with our interactions. Finally, we got on the phone and asked what the problem was. They told us, somewhat abashed, that they got nervous every time they talked to us about logistical details because we would always say, "We've got it handled." Their company, they told us, was driven at a much higher level of distrust about details than was ours. Even though they knew we had it "handled," they expected us to tell them exactly what we had handled, and how. When they felt comfortable that it was handled, they would tell us. That was meeting their expectations. And it was important to them.

But ultimately, long-term relationships are enhanced not simply by meeting expectations, but by exceeding them.

4. Value-Added Service

Value-added service, or constantly exceeding the expectations of customers, is quite simply the best way to improve a relationship continuously. In a partnership, the value-added service has to be built in to the relationship and not left simply to chance.

Heroic vs. Built-In Value

Every company has its stories of employees who went out of their way to serve a customer. Those are the "employees of the month." They get their picture up on the wall for a month, or they get better parking at the office for a week. But that misses the point entirely. Employees should not have to go out of their way to create unexpected value for the customer. It need not take heroic effort, under most circumstances, to exceed the service expectations of customers. It can, instead, be thought out and built in to the jobs, the organization, and the culture.

"Vince Lombardi, the great Green Bay Packers football coach, was my hero. He used to say, 'I don't care if the other team knows what play we're going to run—they're not going to be able to stop us because we're going to execute the play so well.' When it comes to value added, most companies don't have the understanding or the discipline to do all the things that are necessary to continually provide unexpected value to the customer, to execute unexpected value daily. It isn't brain surgery. It's caring for the customer, discipline, and execution."

— Glen Grodem, President and CEO,
Smith Furnishings

The added value shouldn't be "unexpected" from the point of view of the supplier. It needs to be built in to the thinking, planning and execution of all phases of the relationship.

Don't celebrate people going out of their way to serve customers. Instead, eliminate the barriers that keep people from creating unexpected value solutions daily. Put it in job descriptions, make it part of the daily routine.

Write this question in your day planner. Start every day with it: What unexpected value can I add today for the customer?

5. Run toward Problems

A guarantee: there will be problems. There will be big problems and little ones. Customers will be upset with you, And there will be times when everything is going smoothly—but that is an illusion. The reality is that problems are developing but we are just not aware them—yet. Never allow yourself even to think that you won't have problems, because within thirty minutes you will get a phone call: "This is Ellen in shipping and we have a problem with that shipment that your customer needed last Friday. . . . Sorry, it didn't go out."

Partnerships require experts at anticipating, understanding, and solving problems. First, understand that problems never go away. A short Zen story illustrates the point: A man tells a Zen master, "I have a problem." The Zen master says, "I know you have a problem." Startled, the man asks how the master knew he had a problem. The master replies, "Because you have eighty-three problems." "How do you know that?" asks the man. "Because everyone always has eighty-three problems." The man asks, "What am I to do with these problems?" "Solve them," replies the master. "Then you will receive other problems, because everyone always has eighty-three problems." The Zen master then adds, "And there is an eighty-fourth problem: Believing that you shouldn't have eighty-three problems."

That eighty-fourth problem is a big one for many people. But it is in that class of problems like death and taxes, they will never be solved.

All other problems, however, are there for solutions. The first step is changing our mind about what problems are. They are often opportunities in disguise, opportunities to demonstrate responsiveness, creativity, and caring to our customer.

"My philosophy is that you should run toward problems and away from praise. If you run toward problems, they'll never catch you with your back turned."
—Glen Grodem, President and CEO, Smith Furnishings

What is a problem? Take the upset out of it, and a problem is a difference between what someone wants and what he or she has.

Our role as problem solvers is to be expert at understanding—and helping our customers understand—what they want and what they have, and then to close the gap between the two. In a long-term relationship with sometimes complex issues, the keys are to anticipate, to run toward potential problems. Then solve problems with the customer's best interests at heart and, finally, do it creatively.

Anticipate

What can go wrong?

What issues irritate your customer now that could escalate into serious problems?

What are the indicators of potential problems?

What can you do in advance to reduce the probability of problems' happening?

What will you do if it happens?

Positive Intention

What is the best solution for the customer?

How can we turn this problem around to make it a benefit to the customer?

What is the "win-win" solution, where everybody gets what they need?

Creative

Is there a different way to look at the problem?

Can we "get outside of the box" to solve it?

Do we really understand what the customer requires?

Competitive Immunity

Partnering will belong to those people who are comfortable and competent in building long-term relationships. Lone Rangers, used to hit-and-run business, need not apply. The new requirement is to consciously and strategically build relationships by continuously improving all aspects of them. That is how all healthy relationships are sustained.

Immunity: *The state of being protected from or not susceptible to a particular disease or threat.*

When we are effective at building these kinds of partnerships, we create competitive immunity. Competitive immunity means having such a powerful relationship with a customer at all the connecting points that the relationship and the customer are immune from your competition. The switching costs are high; you are seen as indispensable to your customer, *in* business with your customer, not *doing* business with them. That is the goal. So what can you do today to make a difference for a customer? And what will you do tomorrow?

The following are relationship indicators that can help you assess the health of your customer relationship:

PARTNERSHIP INDICATORS

Positive Relationship	Problem Indicator
Initiate positive phone calls.	Make only callbacks.
Make recommendations.	Make justifications.
Use candor in language.	Use accommodating language.
Use the phone to communicate.	Use written correspondence to communicate.
Show appreciation.	Wait for misunderstanding.
Make service suggestions.	Wait for service requests.
Use "we" problem-solving language.	Use "you-us" legal language.
Get to problems.	Only respond to problems.
Use jargon/shorthand.	Use long-winded communications.
Air personality problems.	Hide personality problems.
Talk of "our future together."	Talk about "making good on the past."
Provide routinized responses.	Provide "fire drill"/emergency responses.
Accept responsibility.	Shift blame.
Plan the future.	Rehash the past.

Source: Theodore Levitt, *The Marketing Imagination.* New York: The Free Press, 1983.

Chapter Ten

~~~~~~~~

Driving Business Results

Predicting anything about business over the next few years could be career limiting. But here is a prediction I can guarantee with certainty: economics will be the driving force of the nineties.

In this turbulent, highly competitive decade, customers are seeking significant economic advantage. Your customers are looking for every opportunity to increase profitability and drive out unnecessary cost. The business people who can understand the economics of their customers, and who can create and drive business results for them, will be highly successful in the coming years.

Creating significant economic advantage for customers is the only game played by the individuals and organizations that are serious about keeping customers.

What is new about this approach? It sounds obvious, doesn't it? After all, economics has always driven business. Customers have always looked for an improved bottom line and shopped for suppliers who offered the solution they required at the lowest price. So what is new about the nineties? First, remember the backdrop of increased global competition, rapid technological change, and the commoditization of markets, causing a huge shift in economics for most companies. Now add on an economic reality of our times: the relatively new phenomenon of a *dis*inflationary to flat economy.

In the seventies and eighties, inflation, as awful a dragon as it was, allowed prices to rise, margins to remain stable, and costs to be passed on to the customer. But:

> "As we turned the corner into the 1990s, all that debt was piled on, lots of the equity got cashed in, and inflation was lost as a means to drive growth. Prices were raised, probably ahead of value being raised. As long as the economy was growing, consumers took it in stride. Now, with the economy flat, price competition has increased, and margins have come down. The inflation bandwagon has come to a screeching halt."
> — Mike Szymanczyk, Senior Vice President, Sales, Philip Morris

Yesterday's inflationary economy might be compared to rising water in a swamp—it covered a lot of stumps. It hid all sorts of inefficiencies, duplications, and unnecessary costs. Frankly, badly managed companies could survive as a lack of real competition and inflation covered up lots of waste. Now the water is receding and all the stumps are showing.

Companies are scrambling to figure out how to survive in this strange new swamp: the highly competitive, disinflationary nineties, when you can no longer simply increase prices to increase margins and profits. More than ever before in recent memory, economics are forcing the strategies of businesses, compelling the thinking of top executives. The watchwords are driving out cost, increase margins (without raising prices), and profitability.

What does this mean to a business like yours?

A common assumption is this: the customer will beat us up on price. We will have to give away a lot in order to keep the business.

Here is the dark side of the pressures your customers are under: visions of customers' constantly pressuring salespeople for more and deeper discounts; nightmares of eroding margins on crucial pieces of business.

What Business Are You In?

All true. No use denying it. Customers are swinging a big hammer and the anvil they are gleefully pounding is your price. They want it cheaper! They want it faster, bigger, with more bells and whistles, but they want it cheaper. This is the transactional environment, where price and convenience are the only tools available to the players and they use them as weapons on each other.

Today—maybe in your organization—this debate rages. Salespeople, typically, report back to management ("report back" is a nice, neutral term) that the only way to keep business is to aggressively lower prices, to become the "Wal-Mart" of the industry. Management, on the other hand, tells sales that the only way the company can fund salaries, new products, and the overhead is by holding the line on prices and margins.

It often comes down to this: companies can either be the low-cost provider or a value-added provider. It is difficult to be both. The consequences of being the lowest-cost provider (a business I would never want to be in) is that you are an easy competitive target. competitors need only to beat you on price. It is not a fun business because the margins are so slim that a hiccup in the economy can give you pneumonia.

Being a value-added provider, delivering a greater range value, on the other hand, allows companies to better hold the line on prices. But it all hinges on understanding and delivering the "value added" that customers crave.

Step back and think about what your customers really want. What the customer is looking for—99.9 percent of the time—is economic benefit. Every customer is trying to make money or save money by increasing sales and driving out cost. In most companies, this mandate is tattooed on the consciousness of every employee. As part of that mandate, of course, customers go after suppliers to lower their prices. And why shouldn't they? Suppliers are seen simply as vendors of goods and services, no more and no less.

This is the perception that needs to be changed. It is the leverage point at which a smart organization or individual can significantly change the game for their customer and for themselves. The opportunity involves becoming an invaluable asset to your customers by helping them meet their economic goals, by helping them achieve their business results. Helping your customer hit their business goals happens when salespeople move beyond simply being suppliers of goods and services and take on the role of driving business results.

Driving business results: *Aggressively creating and sustaining significant economic benefit for customers.*

This is the high-level, value-added game of the future. It is the strategic ability that will rapidly launch partnerships and create sustainable competitive immunity.

But it is a different game from the more common one of simply supplying and selling products and services. To feel comfortable and competent in this kind of work requires a high-level understanding of customers, fluency in their financial and business language, and a commitment on your part—and your organization's part—to create and sustain significant economic benefit for your customers.

- Work strategically.

- Speak financially.

- Drive economic benefit.

The Art of the General

> "Working strategically is one of the best ways of outperforming the competition. You have to think in very large strategic terms. You can't outperform the competition by focusing on selling a better price. You have to work on selling quality and the total value and skill package of the corporation."
> — Brian Schmall, James River

Creating this opportunity begins with your view of the playing field. Kenichi Ohmae in *The Mind of the Strategist* described the old model of business that involved three players: you, your customer, and your competitor. This is the field of play for most salespeople. If you diagram this game, it looks like this:

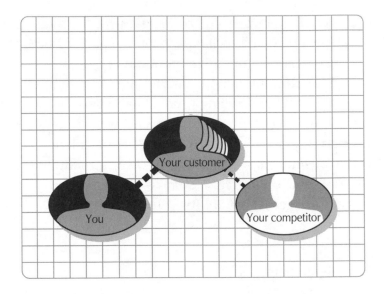

In this game, business is an endless struggle to defeat your competition and win the customer. The tools are product and price. The tactics are cutting prices, using a better sale process, and enticing your customer with higher product value. Energy and effort are used on this business battlefield against the competition. Many businesses and salespeople become trapped in this box, focusing on beating the competition by doing the same kind of business a little bit better.

To make a strategic and highly visible difference for our customers, we have to see a much larger playing field than just you, your customer, and your competitor. In Greek, the word "strategies" means "the art of the general." The prevailing belief was that generals had the view of a larger field and individuals of lesser rank were stuck with a much more limited perspective. Sound familiar?

Driving business results for customers requires first seeing the playing field from the larger perspective of the customer:

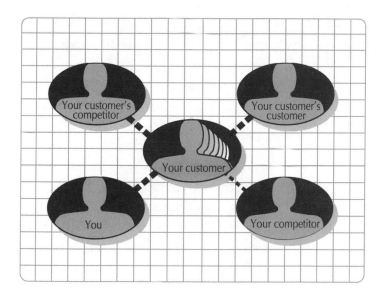

When you see the universe through your customer's eyes, the key players become your customer, your customer's customer, and your customer's competitors. Instead of focusing on how you can beat your competition, working on this larger field revolves around creating competitive advantage for your customers and helping them beat *their* competition—a significantly different game.

> "Over the past ten years, selling has focused on customer satisfaction. But that was always in terms of the customer's need for your product. Now we are having to look much more deeply into our customer's world and needs. We are asking the questions, 'What do our customers need to be more competitive? What do they need to satisfy their customers?' "
>
> — Steven Rauschkolb, Director of Sales and Medical Education, Schering-Plough

A number of new areas of knowledge and expertise go into playing this new game. When your objective is to bring high-level value to a customer, you first need to understand that customer's concerns and opportunities. How do you become steeped in the world of your customer? Of course, doing your homework helps. Subscribe to their industry periodicals, read and clip from the business publications on their industry. Every piece of information that is very important.

But I have gotten further by asking the right people the right questions. Go to school on your customers by taking them to lunch and letting them tell you stories about their business. When you sit down face-to-face with someone, you hear about the business. You discover what keeps people up at night. You find out what is really important and what is just smoke. Do a few such interviews with individuals from all over the spectrum, from inside the companies, with sales-people and executives who sell noncompeting products to your customers. Fairly soon, you will amass a knowledge base that will help you understand what the world looks like through the eyes of your customers.

Business questions

✔ *What business is your customer really in?*

✔ *Who are their competitors?*

✔ *How does your customer make money?*

✔ *How do they lose money?*

✔ *What are their major cost areas?*

✔ *Who are your customer's customers and what do they expect?*

✔ *What keeps your customer up at night?*

✔ *How does your product or service impact your customer economically?*

The answers to these questions constitute the "walking around" information you should have at your fingertips, in your head, or in your laptop. It is the level of understanding that is required to play this more complex game. We toss around the idea of the "niche player." When you are a niche player, you are focused on supplying solutions to a specific industry or customer "niche." Niche players start by having an understanding of their customer's business that can be deeper and broader than the customer's understanding.

NCR Corporation, the AT&T subsidiary, is a good example of this approach. NCR builds and distributes computers. But their niche is the retail environment, and NCR knows as much about the environment as any retailer. As a niche player, NCR brings value to its customers beyond simply selling them hardware because they have focused, studied, and worked in that niche for decades. With this kind of focus on the customer, a salesperson is ready to have a different kind of conversation, one that isn't focused on products, but rather focused on what is truly interesting to the customer: where they are and where they want to go.

The Strategic Conversation

Strategic work is defined by the kinds of conversations you have with customers. What do you talk about? What do they ask you? What do you ask them?

"In the strategic mode, you're looking for opportunities to bring more to the table than just a sale. So you may be asking about a company's long-term growth plans, investment strategies, competitive position, and so on. You're trying to understand the whole picture and make the pie bigger for your customer and your company."
— Tamae Moriyasu, salesperson,
Hewlett-Packard Company

Where Are You Now? Where Do You Want to Go?

Strategic work is based on two questions: "Where are you now?" and "Where do you want to go?" What makes strategic work more complex is who is asking and answering the questions. For example, helping a child choose the right college is a strategic conversation. When I was ready to have that conversation with my parents, "where I was" was that I was five feet six inches and 150 pounds and getting C's and D's in high school. Where I wanted to go was to play football for Notre Dame and then go to medical school. Hmmm. In between where I was and where I wanted to go was the gap—admittedly, a large gap. For General Electric Medical in Wisconsin, "where they were" was a supplier base of forty-five hundred. Where they wanted to go was to a supplier base of fewer than four hundred. In both cases, the strategic conversation begins with those two questions.

In my experience, selling insurance or working with senior executives on quality initiatives, the relationship always turned the corner when my customers began (with my prompting) to open up and talk on this level. They would discuss their frustrations, successes, and the strengths, weaknesses, and threats of "today." Then the imagining-would begin: they would talk about their goals, their visions of the future, where they saw the possibilities and what had to happen to make the possibilities real.

Strip away the "M.B.A. think-tank consultant" trappings and you will discover that strategic-level work is simply this: knowing your customer's business as well as the customer and then in starting this conversation: "Where are you and where do you want to go?"

In a partnership, this conversation will occur frequently with groups of people (all those connecting points!) where the partnership builder, a salesperson or CEO, will need to facilitate the discussion. Often, adding risk and complexity to the equation, the conversation will be with high-level customer executives—they are the individuals who live with the economic equations. They are the ultimate customers of driving business results and the business of partnering will require competency and comfort when dealing at that level.

But don't lose heart, and remember the advantage of working at this level: working strategically means creating partnerships that create competitive immunity. And that is the goal.

"Partnering will require the salesperson to become much more of a resource manager than a salesperson. They will need to understand their customer's business environment and be able to match their corporate capabilities against the needs of the customer.

"That's quite different from making a sales call!

"They will need a thorough—and I mean thorough—understanding of their own business from the organizational perspective, to how products are engineered, services, and what the cost structures are. They will need an understanding of finance, return on investment, because they will be competing for internal dollars. It will require an understanding of the global marketplace. The knowledge and experience of these people will need to be much higher than ever before."

— Rick Canada, Director, Change Management
Services, Motorola

Vital Signs

La lengua del comercia y de la estrategia es financiera. Si usted no comprende esta lengua, no podrá participar en el juego. (Translation: The language of business and strategy is financial. If you can't understand the language, you can't play in the game.)

If you are not practiced at discussing finance, beyond the price and value of products and services, it can be like listening to a foreign language. It doesn't make sense. But to work at this level, to drive business results, you need to speak the language; fluency in finance, in the economic vital signs, is required. In medicine, vital signs are such key indicators of health as level of consciousness, pulse, and blood pressure. Usually, vital signs immediately answer the question, Is this patient healthy or sick? Every doctor, nurse, and paramedic knows how to take and interpret vital signs.

✔ *You can be a salesperson, but you can't build partnerships, you can't drive business results, unless you speak and understand the financial conversation.*

Driving business results requires a fundamental under-standing of financial concepts, fluency in the language of finance, and the ability to read the vital signs and know what they mean. You need to understand what causes pretax profitability for your customer to go up or down. This is the stuff that customers—the high-level ones—live, breathe, and watch daily. That is what they want to talk about, what gets their attention. In the resource section, we've included a summary of some of the key financial vital signs. Remember, you have to speak the language!

The Customer Niche

The objective of all this is to be a niche player in the most important business in your world: your customer's.

The objective is to view your customer as your niche, to be seen by your customer not just as a representative of a product or supplier organization, but as a consultant and an expert in their business. From that deep understanding, large opportunities flow. When you can speak their language, understand their business, and understand what they are trying to accomplish, when you can match that with an understanding of your business and what your company offers, opportunities that would have gone unnoticed will become obvious.

There is another important benefit to being a "niche player." People will work with you, not because they under-stand what you offer, but because they believe you under-stand them. Customers always prefer to work with those who understand their business and are focused on solving their critical business problems, not people who simply want to "push product."

Driving Economic Benefit

With this level of understanding, the mission becomes clear and focused. Think of it this way. If you were on your customer's payroll, your job description would no doubt revolve around one or more of these three key initiatives:

✔ *Make money.*

✔ *Save money.*

✔ *Add value to the customer.*

Of course, we do work for our customers and we need to focus our efforts on the same three initiatives: making money for the customer, saving them money, and adding value to their customers. In the final analysis, these are only things that truly matter. When you are focused and can demonstrate results in one or more of those three areas, you're seen more as partner than vendor. The most important thinking you and your company can do is to identify which of these three initiatives, or combinations of them, you can impact most effectively.

> "When you can help your customers see how you can impact their bottom line by driving cost out of the system, you get their attention immediately. Anybody in business today who is not brain dead will listen."
> — Lou Pritchett, former Vice President, Sales, Procter & Gamble

The goal is to differentiate yourself in the marketplace. Since most organizations are focused on reducing costs, there is usually a lot of opportunity in being seen as an agent for cost reduction. Eliminating waste and streamlining delivery are sure ways to reduce cost to your customer. Simply becoming the most convenient and flexible supplier possible can also lead to a more long-term and profitable relationship for both of you.

✔ *How can you save your customer money?*

✔ *Can you help increase your customer's sales?*

✔ *Can you help add value to their customer?*

Focus on Results

It comes down to this one singular challenge. If you want to be successful, it's important to consistently solve customer problems. If you want to be extremely successful, you need to focus on solving the highest-level business problems of customers. To succeed at this level requires strategic-level thinking and working. It requires an understanding of the financial and business language of your customers and a relentless focus on driving results that either make money, save money, or add value for your customer. It doesn't matter what your customers do or what you sell. If you can make a difference for your customer at this level, you've got a customer for life.

In the next couple of chapters, we will present the tools we use—Discovering Opportunities and the Partnering Process—to help find partnering opportunities and create and implement these kinds of solutions. The success of the Partnering Process depends on the level of play and the vision and understanding of the players. Which is true of all good business processes. The hammer, the saw, and the computer are only as good as the individual using them.

But the most important abilities are willingness to work at a high level, an understanding of the strategic and financial game of customers, and a commitment to creating business results for customers.

Part Four

How to Create a Partnership

M ore than two thousand years ago, in a burst of insight, the Greek mathematician Archimedes allegedly said, to paraphrase: Give me a lever and a place to stand, and I can move the world!—the point being that, with the right tools and the right leverage point, we can accomplish much more than we might think.

Tool: *Instrument or process that makes your job easier and allows you to get more results for less effort.*

Archimedes' enthusiasm has relevance to the business world of today. Given the right tools and the right leverage points, we can accomplish much more with our customers. A good tool magnifies our effect, whether the tool is a screwdriver or an intellectual process. In the business of partnering, the right tools can help you and your customers discover problems and find solutions with less effort.

For example, when I was CEO of Wilson Learning Corporation in the seventies and eighties, we taught salespeople how to use a set of tools that would allow them to leverage their effect in the sales process with a customer. The program was called Counselor Selling; the tools were a step-by-step interactive process that helped a salesperson gain a customer's trust by *relating*; understand the customer's problem by *discovering*; suggest a solution by *advocating*, and respond to objections by *supporting*.

In this section, we are going to introduce a set of tools designed to help identify customers that are potential partners and then identify high-level opportunities with them. These tools can be applied in a one-to-one situation with a customer, or expanded for use in the larger organization-to-organization relationship.

As with all tools that are more complex than a hammer or a screwdriver, practice is essential, and occasionally it will be helpful to refer to the instruction manual. But once the tools become how you do business, you'll find yourself using them habitually and getting more done with less effort.

A Place to Stand . . .

As important to Archimedes as the right tool was a place to stand. In selling, "a place to stand" refers to our perspective, our understanding of what we are trying to accomplish and why. In life, we can't control the circumstances we are presented with, but we can control where we stand, and what we stand for. So the question is, "Where do *you* stand? What is *your* belief about your role and mission regarding your customers?"

Salespeople can be clear and concise when describing their products or services. They can be saying all the right things, nodding attentively while we, as buyers, are talking. Yet, we don't trust them, we perceive them as coming solely from their own agenda—to sell us something. Which is exactly what they are trying to do, and that is the opposite of trying to understand and solve customer problems. That salesperson is not grounded in the role of serving customers.

Being grounded means having a firm and consistent set of beliefs from which our actions spring. It is what we "stand" on. Being grounded in the role of serving customers means we come from the core belief that we are there to help our customers get what they want. Being emotionally and intellectually grounded in understanding and serving customers is more important than the tools or processes we use. It is more important than knowing our products.

Daily, as we drive to work, before we pick up the phone, we need to reaffirm that our purpose in coming to work is to serve our customers and help them get what they want. When you do the right thing for your customers, when you serve them, you are repaid tenfold, long-term. This is the principle that distinguishes the excellent companies from all the rest and the truly excellent salespeople from the mediocre.

Every time we are with them, our customers judge us on how grounded we are, on whether our intention is to meet their needs. They might not do it on a conscious level, they might not give us direct feedback, but they know at an intuitive level why we are there and what our intention is.

As the world becomes more competitive, more companies and new salespeople will be competing for your customers. Every one will be acquiring new skills, new tools and knowledge in order to play in this new game. But as you upgrade, as you learn, as you become more sophisticated, do not forget the most important differentiator: your purpose is to serve your customers, to make a difference for them. Nothing is more powerful than a salesperson grounded and clear in that belief. And when it is combined with the right tools, we can move the world.

Chapter Eleven

〜〜〜〜〜

Discovering Partners

First question, first tool. If you want to develop partnering relationships with customers, whom do you start with? Which customers present the most logical and best opportunities? The fact is that not every customer is ready for, or cares to be involved in, a partnership. There are customers who will simply always buy the lowest price, shopping among several bidders for every piece of business.

Understanding which customers are ready for a partnership is vital information for a couple of reasons. First of all, working at a more complex business level with customers requires (as if you haven't already guessed) a lot of effort and time. Time and effort—unless you can suspend the laws of physics—still are in short supply. Working at this level requires choosing the right opportunities, the right customers. It may also mean letting go of some customers who take up much of your time without producing appropriate results.

Second, since you can't spend the same amount of time and energy on every customer, you have to decide how best to use your resources. The key here is leverage. Leverage means getting as much done as possible, with as little effort as possible. For example, leverage means always getting referrals, because it is easier to call on a referred basis than to call cold. Leverage means continuing to grow existing business, because it is much easier to do business with people who already know you than it is to go out and find new business.

High-level leverage involves knowing where your business comes from and where the natural opportunities lie. Right now, chances are that 80 percent of your revenue comes from about 20 percent of your customers. Using the principle of leverage means focusing the maximum amount of energy where the opportunities lie—with that 20 percent. These are typically the customers who represent large opportunities, who offer the best chance for significantly enhanced relationships.

Finally, one of the blinding flashes of the obvious is that every customer is unique. Some customers buy price, others are more interested in a long-term relationship. Some are truly interested in strategy. But the point is that they are all different; they cannot be treated generically. A common business sin of the past was treating all customers as if they were exactly alike, presenting them with the same products, the same proposals, the same sales process.

> "From a marketing perspective, it used to be that we could give a fairly consistent, focused message to all our customers, because we looked at them as a fairly homogeneous group. Now our customers are really differentiated in what they buy, how they buy, how they want to work with us. Now the messages and the relationships have to be tailored to fit the needs of each customer."
> — Steven Rauschkolb, Director of Sales and Medical Education, Schering-Plough

Increasingly, customers are demanding, and receiving, customized solutions tailored to their specific needs. Customers are individuals, with distinct needs, requirements, and concerns. The generic customer is gone, and so are generic solutions and the "one size fits all" sales process. The best of all worlds is that in which we are versatile enough—as organizations and as individual business people—to match customer requirements with the right products and processes.

Who Is Ready for Partnering?

To answer the question, Which one of these distinct customers is ready for partnering?, let's look at three types of existing buyers. These are broad-brush categories that identify the key motivational factors. Discovering Partners looks at existing buyers in terms of what they want and how they currently do business with us. Again, these categories are broad generalizations. The buyers are as follows:

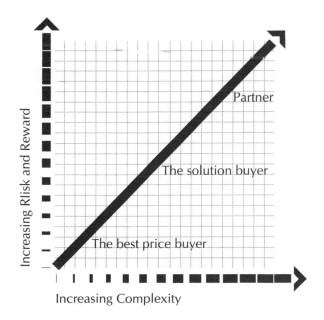

How Much and When? The Best Price Buyer

This customer's motivation for buying is getting the lowest price, and the sale often requires some sort of price concession. The buyer's focus is on buying a prespecified product, and decisions are made on a sale-by-sale (transaction) basis. In a transactional relationship, buyers are not locked into any one vendor and can switch at any time, with little inconvenience to them. It may be relatively easy to get a share of this customer's business for a price, but difficult to develop any long-term loyalty. Margins tend to be low with this type of buyer, and the relationship can often feel adversarial.

Can You Solve My Problem? The Solution Buyer

Solution buyers have somewhat more complex requirements than best price buyers. They are focused on the problem that your product or service solves. In the problem-solving relationship, the buyer and seller invest time, energy, and resources in finding the solution to a defined business problem. This customer is open to creating solutions and exploring options to find the best value for the dollar invested. The revenue stream is more predictable and reliable. The buyer has a vested interest in your support capabilities. Eventually, the buyer will become even more knowledgeable than you about the application and use of your product or service in his environment.

The Partner

The most complex and most profitable relationship, the "holy grail" of keeping customers, is the partner. These customers tend to be well established and committed to buying over a long period of time, recognizing that the business relationship extends beyond any individual product offering. As the buyer and seller grow more dependent on each other, it becomes harder for the customer to switch to another vendor and receive comparable value. It is difficult to see where one organization ends and the other begins. When a partner is lost for any reason, restoring it is difficult and likely to take a great deal of time and effort.

Inside the Mind of the Customer

Five critical questions can help you get inside the mind of the customer and understand what motivates him or her.

The questions work like this: For each of the five questions, assign a score of "0," "1," or "2," depending on which characteristic best describes the customer. When you've completed all five questions, add up the scores. Then use the "Scoring Key" below to classify each customer.

1. What Motivates the Customer's Buying Decisions?

0 = The customer's primary concern is getting the lowest price. The customer views the purchase as a commodity buy with no apparent interest beyond price.

1 = The customer's primary concern is finding ways to reduce costs and at the same time enhance revenue and improve quality. No preset solution exists, and the customer is willing to explore options.

2 = The customer's primary concern is finding new ways to meet *their* customers' expectations and help their customers gain competitive advantage.

2. What Level of Support Does the Customer Require After a Sale?

0 = The customer expects little or no technical assistance or support. The customer already has developed internal technical support and expertise and calls only when the situation warrants.

1 = The customer expects you to provide ongoing technical support and assistance to solve problems.

2 = The customer expects you to create options for expanding and growing new opportunities beyond the purchase of your products. The customer is looking for ongoing support and is open to new ideas for conducting business and responding to customer needs.

3. How Much of the Customer's Total Business Do You Have Compared With Your Competitor's?

0 = You are constantly fighting for a share of the customer's business.

1 = You are the major supplier but not the sole source. The customer is willing to share competitive information and initiatives with you.

2 = You are the sole supplier, and the business relationship clearly extends beyond any individual product offering.

4. How Difficult Is It for Your Customer to Switch to a Competitor?

Switching costs refers to the ease or difficulty with which the customer can shift business to a different supplier. Customers who have made significant investments in people, time, manufacturing processes, or technology to use your products have high switching costs. Those who have no such investments, and no relationship with your organization, have relatively low switching costs.

0 = The customer can easily switch to a competitor at a low cost.

1 = The customer can switch to a competitor at a moderate cost.

2 = The customer can switch to a competitor at a high cost.

5. How Does Your Customer See You?

0 = You are viewed as just another vendor. Contract negotiations are adversarial events. Your primary point of contact is usually limited to the department or individual requesting delivery of a package.

1 = You are viewed as a problem solver. Contract negotiations are collaborative efforts in which you and the customer make compromises and create options rather than engage in hard bargaining to achieve concessions. Your primary contact is at the middle-management or department-head level.

2 = You are viewed as a partner. Contract negotiations focus on structuring an alliance and sharing the gain generated from collaboration. Your primary contact is at the senior management level.

Price, Solution, or Partner?

After you've worked through the five questions, and have assigned a score for each, add up your scores and classify the buying relationship according to this key:

Scoring Key

0–4	Price buyer
5–7	Solution buyer
8–10	Partner

The result is a "howgoesit" picture of your relationship with a specific customer. Obviously, buyers don't neatly fit into categories, but with a touch of intuition and a dash of experience you can assess accurately not only where the relationship is but also where it could go. What is most useful about the Discovering Partners tool isn't the label of best price buyer, solution buyer, or partner, it's the discipline of looking at a customer's motivations through a different pair of glasses. We have found that the discussions generated around the questions can lead to new insights about customers, their needs, and the threats and opportunities that exist.

Once you've put all your key customers through the same question process, you get a snapshot of your business—where your healthy relationships exist, where there are opportunities, and where there are potential problems.

Using the Information

Buying relationships sort out into the Partnership Pyramid. Typically, there are lots of best price customers, fewer solution customers, and just a few customers who are long-term, high-level partners or potential partnership customers.

The Partnership Pyramid

There are two primary uses for the information gleaned from the Discovering Partners exercise. First, it enables you to view customers through the lens of why they buy, which helps you understand what each one expects from you. Armed with that information, you can better leverage your time, energy, and resources.

For example, price buyers want it simple: price and convenience. How do you deliver what they want? How can you make it as convenient as possible for them? How can you use less of their time and still be a valued vendor? Price buyers customers are often perfect candidates for strictly telephone and fax interactions, which take less time while giving them what they want: information about price and convenience.

The second use of the information is to locate and pursue partnership opportunities. Which solution buyers are potential partners, and which partnering relationships can be strengthened? For example, if you have a relationship that is strong in every way except that there are vendors other than you also supplying the customer, your strategy is moving that customer to a single-source relationship. What would you have to do differently? What benefits would have to exist for the customer to consider such a relationship? Each of the five questions represents initiatives that can be used to strengthen the relationship and build on opportunities.

Downgrading, Maintaining, and Upgrading

Ultimately, this is all about matching your best resources with your most important and high-potential customers. For an organization, that might mean reallocating senior people to work with those partnership opportunities, and "letting go" of some less important activities or marginally producing customer relationships. For the individual business person, it means taking a serious look at reevaluating your relationships and making choices about how to use your time and energy.

Here are some suggestions:

Downgrade a buyer relationship if:

- It is low-margin business, considering the time, effort, and resources it requires.

- The relationship is difficult and hard to manage.

- There is a low potential for ongoing business and little potential for elevating the buying relationship from best price buying to problem solving.

- If you could choose, you would prefer your competition to have the account because of the high cost of time and resources.

Don't misunderstand: "downgrading" doesn't necessarily mean dumping the business or treating some customers as if they are not as important as others. It does means working with the customer in a way that is most appropriate.

Maintain the relationship if:

- The customer is a high-quality, high-margin business that is predictable and can be accurately forecasted.

- The account has the potential to produce a steady and stable revenue stream.

- The buyer shares intentions openly, and mutual reliance and mutual benefit are derived from the relationship.

- The buying relationship is open and can be characterized as "easy to sell to, a pleasure to do business with."

- The buying relationship has the potential to evolve into a partnering relationship at a later date.

Grow the relationship if:

- The buying relationship with this customer is well established, highly visible, and important to your revenue stream.

- There is a high probability of incremental revenue.

- Combined resources can be leveraged from the buyer and your organization that result in new products, new business, entry into new markets, and increased competitive advantage for both organizations.

Readiness Reality

The great thing about writing a book is that you get to sit in your home with a cup of coffee and a computer and describe how things should work in theory. In theory, you and your customers will be ready at the same time to create new and different kinds of relationships. In theory, your resources, how you use your time and energy, align perfectly with what your customers expect and need. In theory. But, of course, reality doesn't work that way. The reality is that you have to do your best with the information you have, the hand you are dealt, and the talents you've been given. A little luck helps, and timing is everything.

Reality also suggests that success and luck favor those who are prepared. Understanding your customer prepares you for the opportunities that timing and luck might bring. In business, knowing where the opportunities are and where they aren't is valuable information. Discovering Partners is a leverage tool (more results for less effort) that helps you discover opportunity and prepares you and your organization to find relationships that could be remarkably profitable for both parties.

Chapter Twelve

~~~~~~

The Strategic Partnering Process

> "My best friend, Dr. A. C. Rolen of Bristol, Tennessee, collects old golf clubs. He has tried his best to use a 1910-era club to drive a ball as far as he can with a brand-new 'state of the art' Ping club, but he only gets about half the distance. Similarly, you can't use antiquated tools to deliver to the new customer, supplier, or partner. They just won't work."
>
> — Lou Pritchett, former Vice President, Sales, Procter & Gamble

Anyone who spends time with customers on a regular basis has a mental map, a sales process, that guides them through the various stages of a business relationship. The process keeps them on track toward a goal and helps them anticipate issues and concerns that inevitably pop up. Let's consider this scenario. You've discovered a customer that is interested in taking their relationship with your company to a higher level. There is clearly a meeting of the minds, all agree that there is probably economic benefit to be had. Now, everyone is looking to you to take charge, to make this partnership happen. What are you going to do? What road map will you follow to take your company and your customer to this new territory called partnership? What are the state-of-the-art tools that discover and drive business results?

Creating partnerships—the most sophisticated of buyer-seller relationships—will require a new road map and a different role for the individuals doing the work of creating partnering relationships.

I've learned this from experience. At Pecos River Learning Centers, we routinely bring together supplier organizations and customer organizations to create partnerships. We play the role of the "midwife," there to keep things on track, to nudge the process forward, and help keep everyone focused on the potential benefit of the relationship. The road map we follow is called the Strategic Partnering Process, the role we play is that of consultant and facilitator.

Facilitate and Consult

Most dictionaries define "consultant" as someone you go to in search of guidance or expert advice. Customers of consultants are looking for help in understanding problems and opportunities or in solving problems. Consultants don't try to "sell" their clients anything; they assist them in understanding or in seeing things differently.

The "tools" of consultants are often simply systematic approaches to solving problems. For example, a medical consultant, the ER doctor, has a process that he or she uses every time to diagnose the problems of a patient. Does the patient have an open airway? Is the patient breathing? Is the patient conscious? From that process, the doctor can efficiently and effectively discover the problems that exist and then create solutions.

Facilitate: *To make easier or less difficult; help forward.*

The second element of the role of creating partnerships is facilitating. Those same "partnership" consultants are able to take complex information and conflicting opinions and make sense of them. They use process tools that make it easier for customers to understand and solve problems.

Who Should Be Involved?

The role is to consult with your customer and your company on creating a partnership. The next question is, Who needs to be involved? The answer: All the "stakeholders" in this potential partnership—everyone potentially impacted by it.

Partnerships require senior executive commitment from both organizations to provide permission and protection; they also require involvement from the people closest to the products, the problems, and the daily work of the relationship.

A good illustration of this was the partnership we mid-wifed between DuPont Fibers and a large East Coast textile manufacturer DuPont supplied with raw materials. The week-long partnership session—the first in the history of their relationship—brought together people who actually worked on the production lines at both DuPont and the textile company.

During the meeting, many large issues were discussed. But they also got down to the specifics that only the line workers understood. The textile line people said that their job would be a lot easier if they could reduce the amount of "fuzz balls" (they are exactly what you imagine) that occasionally surfaced in DuPont Fibers' textile runs. The simple solution was a dedicated telephone line connecting the customer's manufacturing floor with the floor of the DuPont plant. With direct communication (instead of through the glacial-pace chain of command), the textile line workers can call the DuPont line workers as soon as fuzz balls begin to appear, and DuPont can correct the problem immediately. Next, the two groups discussed the size of the rolls that DuPont shipped. The textile plant workers said that their jobs would be a lot easier if, instead of twelve-inch or fourteen-inch rolls, DuPont would send ten-inch roles. After a moment's thought, the DuPont plant spokesman said, "We can do that. We just never knew that was what you wanted."

Solutions are created by the people close to the problems. When you embark on a problem-solving process with a customer, as many stakeholders in the problem as possible should be involved.

The First Step: Establishing Trust

Once the stakeholders have been identified, the critical first step is to make sure that trust exists among the players. Remember, I trust you when I believe that you have my best interests at heart. Indicators that trust exists between businesses are the following:

■ *Immediate problem solving.* Anytime individuals from the buyer organization are dissatisfied with you, your product, technical support, or any other aspect of the relationship, they communicate with you immediately.

■ *Frequent contact.* There is frequent contact between you and the buyer—or between organizations—especially about complaints, concerns, or emerging situations.

■ *Honest communication.* Communication is honest and frank, with few, if any, hidden agendas.

■ *High and wide relationships.* The relationship is not limited to one individual or department in each organization. Each company has immediate access to decision makers and the ability to call "high and wide" in the other company.

It is just not possible to create partnership without a high degree of trust. When we "midwife" partnerships, our focus is on building the relationship first, giving all the participants an experience of what it would be like to work in an environment high in trust. A partnership, or any relationship where high-level, sensitive information is shared, will not survive in a hostile or even apathetic environment. Remember, most relationships between buyer and supplier have a touch or more of "adversarialness." To move into new territory and achieve higher levels of collaboration, distrust has to shift to trust, defensiveness to openness, and blaming to problem solving.

Once there is a foundation of trust, mountains can be moved. With the right people involved, and with high levels of trust, the Strategic Partnering Process can rapidly leverage the relationship into a partnership. The process is highly flexible; it can be done with a customer one-to-one, or expanded to a comprehensive process involving teams over a period of months.

The Strategic Process: GSE=VAO=SER

The Strategic Partnering Process is designed to help *gather, sort,* and *enhance* information leading to the discovery of *value-added opportunities* that, when implemented, create *significantly enhanced relationships* with customers.

The process asks six key questions:

Step 1. Where are we now? (*Situation analysis.*)

Step 2. What's important to the buyer and to us? (*Critical issues and implications.*)

Step 3. What's possible? (*Future perfect scenario.*)

Step 4. What do we need to do? (*Strategies.*)

Step 5. Who? What? When? How? (*Tactics.*)

Step 6. How will we know when we're there? (*Measurement.*)

Step 1: Where Are We Now? (Situation Analysis)

The process of discovery—and understanding what you have discovered—is the most important step in the Strategic Partnering Process. In this "detective" phase, the mission is to collect, sort, and enhance information. Out of the situation analysis come the understanding and insight that are the prerequisites to meaningful action.

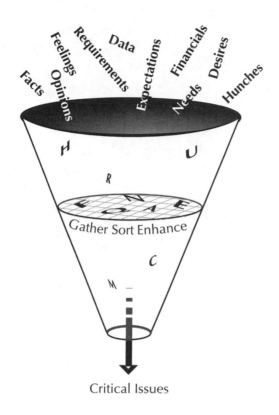

Critical Issues

Insight: *An instance of apprehending the true nature of a thing, especially through intuitive understanding.*

The situation analysis has three components: gathering, sorting, and enhancing information.

Gathering information is simply that—gathering all the relevant information about the problem you seek to solve or the relationship with the customer. First, do your homework. Learn as much as possible about the customer, their industry, and their specific issues. Much of this information is at your fingertips if you have a personal computer and a modem. We regularly use the business databases from Compuserve and

America On-line to fill in the blanks about customers and industries. This is especially helpful when you are dealing with medium to large organizations.

After you've done your homework, the next basic means of gathering information is interviewing: sitting down with the key players, either one-to-one or in a group, and getting their input and insights about the situation. Interview—at least—the following buyers in the customer organization:

■ *The economic buyer.* The person responsible for determining and approving the economic benefit of an enhanced relationship.

■ *The concept buyer.* The individuals who understand your products and services conceptually. This is often the person who was your original "internal advocate."

■ *The end user.* The people in your customer's organization who use your products or services.

■ *The customer's customer.* Somewhere across the value chain there is a customer of your customer that is impacted by what your company supplies. How can the partnership positively impact them? What are their issues and concerns?

Gathering, Sorting, Enhancing: The Interviews

The interview process that we use can be done with one buyer or a cross-cut of the different "stakeholders" from a buying organization.

The process involves three steps.

Gathering Expectations. The first step is to discover the customer's specific expectations. Your goal is to generate a list of everything the customer expects from you, including quality levels, service levels, and shipping times.

Sorting Priorities. The next step is to ask the customer to prioritize. Which expectations are most important? What are the needs that, if unmet, could cause serious damage? What are the least important items? What are the items that are not actual customer requirements, but simply requests? Minimizing back orders might be a customer requirement, while being accessible by voice mail is a request. High priorities tend to be requirements; low priorities tend to be requests.

Enhancing Information. So far, this is valuable information, but it doesn't provoke immediate action. The crucial third step, enhancing information, is the one that usually points to opportunities. Ask your customer to rank your performance on the listed items. On a scale from 1 to 5, with 1 the highest and 5 the lowest, how are you doing on meeting expectations? Where are the problems? Where are you performing adequately? Where are you performing exceptionally?

Once this process is completed, you will have four categories of information:

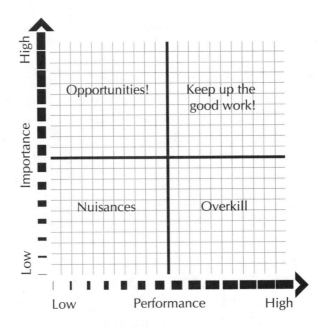

A. *Opportunity Areas.* The buyer perceives the problem as important, but your ability to solve the problem as low.

An opportunity area, for example, would be when the end-user buyer requires deliveries to be made each morning by 6:30 A.M., but your delivery schedule has been erratic or based on your company's delivery schedule.

Action: *Improve performance rapidly!*

B. *Maintenance Areas.* The buyer believes the problem is important and that you are doing good work.

For example, your customer expects custom packing on premium-priced surgical trays, which is exactly what you deliver.

Action: *Keep up the good work.*

C. *Overkill?* The buyer doesn't believe the problem is important and wonders why you are working so hard in the area.

Your company has made an all-out effort to have all the customer representatives on twenty-four-hour pagers, but for the past year, a customer has never paged anyone after business hours.

Action: *Reevaluate energy and resources used to meet these expectations.*

D. *Nuisances.* The buyer perceives the problem as a low priority and doesn't believe that you can solve it.

The buyer that you supply furniture to wishes that you would remove the tags that say, "Don't remove under penalty of law"—but you can't.

Action: *Reevaluate energy and resources used to meet these expectations.*

From this process emerge the important buyer issues. Additional valuable information is your organization's ability to act on those expectations that are highly important to the customer. If the customer ranks an expectation as high and you assess your performance ability as low, you've got a problem!

This basic process can be done with one buyer, with the information gathered on the back of an envelope. Or you can apply the same process to help customer groups prioritize expectations together, a powerful process that quickly creates a list of critical and important issues for the supplier.

Step 2: What's Important to the Buyer and to Us? (Critical Issues and Implications)

Question: What's important?

The goal is to uncover three to five critical issues (more than that can become unwieldy) that are important to the buyer and that you and your organization can impact. Equally important is understanding the implications of the issues.

■ What are the consequences if nothing changes?

■ How will that affect the relationship?

■ How will it affect your customer's ability to make money, save money, or add value?

■ What is the actual dollar cost associated with the current situation?

Understanding and getting agreement on critical issues and implications will provide a sense of the buyer's "fever" for change. It also creates concrete issues that can be discussed, solved, and measured.

Step 3: What's Possible?
(Future Perfect Scenario)

Vision: *The ability to perceive something not actually visible, as through mental acuteness or keen foresight. A power or force of imagination.*

Question: What's possible?

The future perfect scenario plants the seed, allows all the stakeholders to imagine what the future would look like if the partnership handled the critical issues. "If we had Just-in-Time delivery, and zero defects from your organization, we would save $100,000 each quarter in system costs." "If I invested all my funds with your firm, I would only have to talk to one person, but I still would have the diversification that I need."

The value of this step is that it pulls people out of the brush fires and problems of the moment and helps them taste, feel, and experience what a perfect future partnership could be like. The future perfect scenario emerges as a result of these questions:

- If we solve the problems, if we address the critical issues, what would it look like?

- How would it change the relationship?

- How would it save us money, make money, or add value to the customer's customer?

The future perfect scenario involves creating a shared vision, a consensus among team members regarding their desired mutual future. It includes a conceptual image of what the relationship will look like, and fleshes out the details that will be required to make it possible.

The Future Perfect Process

A. *Brainstorming.* First, have the participants—your customers and people from your organization—generate mental snapshots of what the future perfect vision looks like. This is brainstorming, and the objective is to generate lots of ideas—no holds barred. What does our future look like if we solve the critical issues? Be specific: no lofty statements or glittering generalities. Instead, focus on goals that are attainable, agreed upon, and—important for later on—measurable.

For example: "As a result of this partnership, we will reduce operating costs by 5 percent within one year" is a measurable goal. If it's attainable and agreed upon, it is a future perfect statement. It also specifies a reasonable time period (one year) that allows for the kinks to have been worked out and the critical issues operationally addressed.

It is also important to imagine the relationship. In this future perfect scenario, how are we treating each other? What does it feel like to be part of the team, the partnership, or the group that is solving an important problem for the customer? What do individuals see, hear, and feel as they imagine the highly successful partnership one year from now?

B. *Organizing the Ideas.* Next, organize the ideas into clusters under broad themes. These will eventually become the elements of the vision. A good way to start is by placing the ideas from the visioning exercise into two categories:

■ *The business issues.* The financial or productivity implications of meeting the goals and solving the critical issues.

■ *The relationship issues.* How are we treating each other?

How open is the relationship? Is information flowing freely? Are decisions made with a minimum of bureaucratic interference? Are we solving problems together? Are our core values aligned?

Again, strive for specific and concrete language. At this point, you're looking for behaviors that support the theme rather than abstractions. Here are some examples that might emerge:

"We notify each other immediately when there are problems."

"We hold discussions four times a year to monitor levels of satisfaction and measure progress."

"We have quarterly celebrations of successes."

Once several themes have emerged, the next step is to write a compelling phrase describing each theme. The themes should be concrete and achievable. Once the themes are wordsmithed, they can be combined to form the "future perfect vision" statement. It shouldn't be longer than a paragraph.

The Road to Singapore

An example of how the future perfect scenario can drive decision making and action came from a large petrochemical customer of ours who decided to open a plant in Singapore in order to compete with the Japanese in their own backyard. The organization estimated the cost of the start-up to be approximately $200 million. The next step was getting people to relocate. Everyone understood the old relocation game, which was "You're moving to Singapore." On the home front, this translated to: "We're moving to

Singapore. Sell the house, pack the kids, and I'll see you in three months when you get there."

But this corporation decided to change this game. First, they *asked* people if they wanted to go and respected and supported their choices, whatever they turned out to be. Next, they gathered those employees who agreed to go together with their spouses and the contractors who would be responsible for building the plant. Over four days, the "stakeholders" created a future perfect scenario of the experience, first for themselves and their families, and then for the company. Great care was taken to balance personal growth, professional growth, and family life in the vision.

After that session, they had one year to develop their plan. They started by looking at how the company's plants had been built in the past. It became clear that the old way, which included all kinds of highly redundant systems, was too expensive to compete successfully on the Pacific Rim. So they started over with a blank sheet of paper. The new plan dropped some of the old "we've always done it that way" redundancies and incorporated some new risks. But they were risks that needed to be taken if the plant was to be successful.

In drafting the plan, team members kept their eyes on the vision they were trying to create. As a result, the plan was $50 million under the original estimate. It was approved and they are on their way.

Nothing is quite as compelling as a powerful vision of what could be. Under its influence, people are motivated to take those first steps of the journey because they see what is possible, what it is going to feel like and look like, and what they will be doing when they get there.

Step 4: What Do We Need to Do? (Strategies)

> "Only ideas that we actually live by are of any value."
> — Hermann Hesse

Question: What do we need to do?

With the future perfect firmly in mind, the question becomes, How are we going to get there? Start with strategies first. Strategies are the broad initiatives, the campaigns that set out the general direction of the plan without the minutiae of a comprehensive and detailed plan. For example, "Improving our customer-response time 10 percent per year for the next three years" is a broad strategy. It describes where we are going and when we will get there, but it doesn't give the details.

To keep the process manageable, an initiative should be limited, initially, to three to five broad strategies. Human and organizational natures being what they are, fewer strategies mean a higher probability of things getting done.

Here are some questions to answer as you develop strategies:

■ What are the highest-priority items?

■ What are the obstacles to getting what we want?

■ What supports us in obtaining what we want?

■ What actions will be required to overcome the obstacles?

■ What resources and support will we need from others?

■ How are we going to enroll the appropriate people?

Step 5: Who? What? When? How? (Tactics)

Each strategy needs to be translated to answer the question "What do you want me to do right now?" Whereas strategies are general, tactics are as specific as required by the persons or teams doing the work. Tactics are work assignments. Good work assignments need to be flexible and take their audience into account. Some people are comfortable with assignments like "Figure this out by next week." Others need unambiguous, step-by-step marching orders. In any case, as the partnership divides up tasks, it's important that each assignment defines the basics: who, what, when, and how.

Step 6: How Will We Know When We're There? (Measurement)

As a general rule, never enter into any partnership in which results cannot be measured. Without measurability in hard, usually financial data, any relationship, regardless of the "future perfect," will not survive. This is especially true of partnerships. Since they exist to increase the long-term profitability of organizations and individuals, their results need to be published, defensible, and agreed upon.

The parties should agree in advance on how to measure results. Ask, "How will we know if we've succeeded?" Go back to the situation analysis. What were the key indicators, the critical success factors for your partner? How were those indicators expressed? In dollars? Percentage of revenue? Reject rates? At the core of almost every important issue is something to measure. The key principles are to make sure that the goals to be measured are agreed upon, obtainable, quantifiable, and as simple as possible!

Agreed upon:

For example, everyone involved in the partnership agrees that a 5 percent reduction in delivery delays is required for the partnership to be successful.

Obtainable:

There is an excellent probability that, given all the known factors, the goal can be reached.

Quantifiable:

Try to measure what is easily measurable. Dollar amounts, time gained, or defect rates are easier to measure than "satisfaction" or employee involvement. Sometimes, you are stuck with having to measure less concrete variables; but try first to discover the most measurable factors.

Celebrate!

Never allow a chance to celebrate a success pass by. Once a goal is accomplished, even a small one, publicly honor and celebrate it. Whether you throw a party or simply send a congratulatory memo, celebration supports, reinforces, and acknowledges people. When we are supported and acknowledged for doing the right things, we tend to keep on doing them.

The Kodak black-and-white film division radically reorganized from vertical silos to a system known as "flow," a highly interdependent organization focused on the customer. Team Zebra, as they called themselves, used celebration extensively to reward the achievements of individuals and teams. They had Zebra parties, they made Zebra theme songs and awards. Hard work, paradigm busting, and celebrating became the culture of the Zebra team. Their success was a testimony to the power of letting people "reinvent" the organization as well as the power of celebrating and rewarding those people.

Now What? Shake It, Break It, and Remake It!

In a true partnership, there is no end point. Once the Strategic Partnering Process objectives have been met, the process starts over again. What is the current situation? What are the new critical issues? How can we get better?

The Strategic Partnering Process is the tool that leverages your ability to create significantly enhanced relationships with your best customers. It gives structure to the process of developing partnerships. After using it a few times, it becomes habit—it becomes how you tinker with the system, how you automatically attack problems. It is a process that keeps the relationship healthy, alive, and always improving. The switching costs keep going up, the competitive advantage for both organizations increases, and that is truly the bottom line.

Chapter Thirteen

~~~~~~~~

Preparing for the Weather

We have taken a fast ride through our vision of the future of the business, from the "big picture" perspective of permanent white water to specific tools that can help you create the partnerships of the future.

Yet, all of this is simply information. We believe that the information in this book represents a premier strategy for creating amazingly powerful and successful relationships with customers. The future of business lies in creating partnerships. The future involves tearing down the barriers that have separated suppliers from customers in order to work together instead of working at odds.

And we are firmly convinced that Playing to Win, working in teams, building long-term relationships, and driving business results for customers will make the difference between surviving in this new world and truly thriving. Finally, these strategic abilities are for everyone in the organization—not just salespeople. *Everyone* needs to play in the game of keeping customers. That is the most important business lesson that we are relearning today.

But this is simply our perspective, based on our information. And information is useless unless it is energized with creativity and courage.

And that, of course, is up to you. The information presented here is not as important as your ability to use your courage and creativity in order to create what you want. You are just as capable as I am of looking around, seeing how the world is changing, and acting on that information. You are fully capable of sitting down with your best customer and saying, "I don't want to sell you anything anymore; I want to help you reach your goals and help you solve your important problems."

This is easy for me to say. I have been in front of customers for nearly half a century, and long ago came to the realization that what is important in this world is to be ourselves, to use our courage and creativity to help others get what they want. Nothing is more fulfilling. So that is what I concentrate on when I am at my best.

A lot of this comes with the perspective of age and experience. When you are starting out in business, it is easy to be caught up in the awards, in competing and winning, in being the best in your division or your company. For salespeople, it is easy to get stuck on the idea that selling is about beating quotas, winning trips, making a lot of money. In that mindset, serving customers often takes a backseat.

But this is all like the proverbial meteor in a summer sky. It burns brightly for a instant but soon disappears. If you cannot discover other reasons for working, if you've hooked your self-worth to that fleeting bright light in the sky, I can assure you that you will also fade out. That motivation will not illuminate your life and work for the long haul.

If you talk to experienced, successful, and fulfilled people, people who have been out there for a long time Playing to Win, you learn that money and competing are not the items that turn them on. What illuminates their lives is knowing they are making a difference, knowing they are adding value to people around them.

And here is the closely held secret shared by a relatively

few outrageously happy and fulfilled people: when you are truly engaged in helping others, the money is not that important.

Don't get me wrong, money is a good thing! It is wonderful to make a lot of money. It is good to earn money to buy nice things, to have security, to take care of your family. But it is not the secret of life. It cannot, for example, pay you back in kind for all the years of working hard and missing the soccer games, the school conferences, and just the time playing with your kids.

But when we focus on serving, on using our talents to help others, then money is put in the right perspective. It is no longer the goddess that we worship and are often enslaved by. And that is freeing, that is empowering.

So think about it. Focus on who you want to be, not what you want to have. When you look back, what would you want your life to have been about? Having new cars, a big house, being the number-one sales rep in your company? Or do you want your life to have been about making a difference for those you work and live with? We are all here to do important and meaningful work. Not to do so is a waste of your limited and precious time.

But the choice is up to you. If you want to be among the few who are fulfilled and excited about the business of finding and keeping customers, make it your purpose to serve your customers. Follow that purpose and be passionate about it. There are not enough people in business who are passionate about customers, and it is refreshing to run across the few who are.

What Are You Thinking About Today?

A passion for serving customers will serve you in the long run—that is true business folk wisdom that has survived for centuries. But there is also "rattling and shaking" going on today. Events are careening by us. The current we are caught in is turbulent and powerful. What gave us a competitive advantage yesterday turns into a commodity used by everyone tomorrow. You cannot rest on past successes; you constantly need to be innovating, pushing the envelope, changing what you do and then changing again.

Mike Szymanczyk of Philip Morris summed it up one afternoon while we were talking about our favorite topic, business. We were sitting on a deck overlooking the Pecos River, which was in full spring flow, glittering off the rocks and foaming through the rapids below. Mike said that if you get out of bed in the morning thinking that your job today is to do exactly what you did yesterday, then you've missed the boat. Everyone, every day, needs to keep a weather eye on the future and play a part in inventing what the future looks like. That is everyone's daily responsibility, a daily contribution to the business.

Yes, everyone in a business needs to produce results. Most businesses want their employees to keep their noses to the grindstone, especially in tough times. But everyone in the business, in those same tough times, also needs to be part of imagining the future.

Besides doing our jobs, we all need to be continually improving—breaking, shaking, and remaking—those same jobs.

This is vital for all our businesses. The employees—empowered, creative, knowledgeable about customers—are key to an organization's ability to reinvent itself and to create partnerships.

Our friends at Baxter Healthcare told us a story that re-reinforces how fast change is taking place in the marketplace of ideas. A senior sales team from Baxter was going in to call on an important industrial customer. They were prepared with their strategy and their sales presentation, and in the back of their minds, they no doubt also had their quotas firmly affixed. But as soon as they sat down, their customer held up a sign on which the international symbol for "stop" was superimposed on the word "selling":

The customer told the Baxter people he wanted them to stop selling, stop trying to sell him stuff, because they had much more important work to do together. There were important problems to solve *together*, like driving out material costs and inventory costs. This customer wanted to create a new kind of relationship in which buyer and seller would sit on the same side of the table, rather than face each other in their historically adversarial roles. If they were willing to work at that level, they would win, because he would win. He wanted change and he wanted it now.

So the question, of course, is will you be ready, will you have the solutions, the knowledge, and the ability to adapt when your best customer puts the "Stop Selling" sign in front of you? Will you be ready if it happens tomorrow, or next week, or next quarter? Because it will happen. That is the direction we are moving in. That is the flow of the river.

Your Role: Change Agent

So it comes down to this. What role do you want to play? We are often asked this question: What should I do to change, what should I do to prepare my organization for the future?

The probable truth is that roles and titles like CEO, sales manager, and salesperson are meaningless and becoming obsolete in the larger business landscape. They no longer reflect the work that has to be done in most companies. They no longer reflect the degree of collaboration that needs to occur.

Even the traditional idea of the organization—that powerful entity with a life of its own—is obsolete. There is no such thing as an "organization," nothing that you can touch and say, this is Apple Computer, Aetna, or General Motors. Instead, there are collections of people, ideas, and resources. Companies (or marriages, families, communities, or countries) are powerful when all those people are in alignment and working together toward the same goal. Disasters occur when everyone is going in different and divisive directions.

Most organizations are yearning for individuals who can bring them together, focus them on the future, and give them permission and help to change. We call these unique individuals "change agents." They are people who understand change, embrace change, and make change easy for others. Change agents are not stuck in the mud of the problems of the present. They lead groups of people into the future.

Change agents are found all over the organization, from the CEO to salespeople. When there are enough change agents in a group of people, they create excitement and passion for change. They can help that group, be it a community or a corporation, create the future.

When you think about your role, think in larger terms than changing to become more successful for yourself. Think about becoming a change agent for others. Think of serving your customers and your collection of people as an agent of change.

Living with the Weather

Let's go back to the always unpredictable, often lousy weather. Remember, there is really no such thing as bad weather, there are simply unprepared people. If this book, even in a small way, helps you prepare for the weather, for the future of working with customers, it will have served its purpose. The key to the future is to not get caught unprepared, to be ready for whatever is thrown at us.

This seems like a contradiction. If the future is basically unpredictable, how can you prepare for it? By being open to it, being willing to change. It means being willing to take on the position of the learner, willing to try, willing to make mistakes in the pursuit of knowledge and understanding. All this is part of the journey of learning and growth.

It is like, of course, our children. They are relentless in the pursuit of natural learning, willing to make mistakes, and accepting of the scrapes and bruises that come with the territory. Children are rarely tied to the past. They face the future with the excitement of a painter facing a blank canvas, seeing limitless possibilities rather than empty space. So our common task, as we face our future, is to become again like children, open to the future and to whatever it might throw at us.

The forecast predicts that the future will throw unpredictable and exciting times at us; full of possibilities. We will need raincoats, sunglasses, life preservers, and wings. But we can't get caught in the trap of believing that the future in this business will be just like the past.

Right now—today—you have customers dreaming about throwing out all the old selling baggage, customers who will be ecstatic about creating partnerships with you, who will be excited about having you on their team. They will need a nudge in the right direction, and they will need your help in overcoming the obstacles that exist. But the potential and promise are there, yours to grasp.

When does it begin? With your next call on that important customer. With your next drive into work wondering, How can I make a difference? That's when the future begins for me. I began this book by writing that I had been a salesperson for forty-five years and that I was proud of that fact. Let me end by saying how excited I am about the prospect of the future. My invitation to you is to join me in becoming a change agent to create the future of business. I promise you it will be an exciting and fulfilling ride, worth the risk. As always, the future is ours to invent and ours alone to create.

Resource
Section

Tools for Playing to Win

Five Steps to Creating Your Future

The first essential in creating a Playing to Win life strategy is to decide what you stand for and what you want in your life and future. This five-step plan will help you organize that information.

1. Values and talents

Values are those ideals, principles, standards, and morals that create our life priorities, which in turn affect our decisions and choices.

> ✔ *What are your values? What do you stand for?*
>
> ✔ *What are the principles that you will not compromise?*

Talents are those physical and mental strengths and abilities that we are good at. We are born with them or we learned and developed them. How do you know when you are talented at something? It usually feels natural and easy. Talents make it easy and fun for us to accomplish certain tasks, to make things happen and get things done.

> ✔ *What are your talents? What are you good at? What do you enjoy doing?*

2. Life purpose

Our life purpose is the reason we are here. It is what we commit our life to, bigger than ourselves, using our unique talents. It is part of the underlying motivation and driving force that guides our actions and brings us fulfillment. It helps us rise above daily concerns and compels us to make a difference in our lives and the lives of others. A life purpose is not a specific goal, but rather a lifelong process that can be lived regardless of our circumstances or situation.

✔ *What is your life purpose?*

An effective life purpose statement is:

- Clear and concise, no longer than two or three sentences
- Simple to understand and remember, compelling and inspirational
- Congruent with our values and talents
- Attainable by our efforts alone, regardless of outside forces

3. Develop a personal vision

If our life purpose statement describes why we do what we do, a personal vision statement describes what we want our future to look like. It is a dream of how we want things to be. A personal vision statement answers two questions: "What will I be doing?" and "What will it feel like?"

✔ *What is your personal vision for your life? What do you see yourself doing if you are living your life purpose?*

An effective personal vision statement:

- Has short, clear sentences in the present tense detailing specific actions—e.g., "I have earned my M.B.A.," "I am a new manager in my department," "I have positive personal relationships with my customers," "I am taking more risks."

- Excites our imagination and inspires us to act.

- Is congruent with our values, talents, and life purpose.

4. Create a developmental plan

What do you need to do in order to achieve your vision? What specific steps would be required? These improvements should be accomplished within one year, if possible, and be of such a nature that you're willing to ask others for support in achieving them.

- First, identify a fear that is presently keeping you from achieving your vision.

- Identify a skill at which you are currently competent, that you want to master in the coming year. To identify mastery, benchmark yourself against the best in this competency. Choose a competency that, when mastered, will help you achieve your vision.

- Identify a skill at which you are not currently competent but want to become competent in during the next year and which will help you reach your vision.

5. Identify obstacles and support

What are the obstacles you need to overcome to get what

you want and achieve your vision? What support do you need to help overcome the obstacles?

This master plan will help clarify what you stand for and what you want in your life. But there are no tricks or shortcuts. Creating the blueprint is the first, and arguably the easiest, step. Living the plan and overcoming the obstacles are what Playing to Win is all about.

How to Climb the Pole

The next step in Playing to Win is to become skilled at handling the problems, great and small, that come at us every day.

Imagine that you're looking straight up at twenty-five feet of telephone pole. You're harnessed in, the safety lines are checked, and you are ready to climb. You're anxious, your heart is beating rapidly, you feel somewhat weak in the knees. Part of you is saying, "Don't do this!" Another part seeks the adventure.

Sound familiar? When you are choosing between Playing to Win or Playing Not to Lose, you often find yourself in such situations. In climbing poles of any kind, the key is to rapidly engage our rational thinking when we are hit in the head with challenge, change, and fear.

Stop!

The first thing we can do when faced with challenge or a choice is to stop for a moment, calm down, take a couple of deep breaths (seriously, it works, just like your mom told you when you were five years old!). It is critical to intervene physiologically first by controlling your breathing. Slow, deep breathing helps you relax. The more relaxed you are, the better you are able to think rationally instead of reacting emotionally.

Challenge!

The next step is to challenge any irrational thinking that is producing feelings of fear and anxiety. Often, faced with a problem, we immediately begin to make up stuff about it. We *add on* to the problem. A few common "add-ons" are:

- *Denial.* We deny that there is a problem, hoping it will just go away.

- *Awfulizing.* We "make up" that the problem is worse than it actually is.

- *Blaming.* We find a target for our anger and we play "He did it, she did it, they did it." Rarely does blame solve a problem, but it takes up a lot of energy.

- *Overlooking the benefit.* We fail to see the growth possibilities, the nugget of gold amid the rubble.

- *Connecting the problem to self-worth.* This is a killer. We make a problem or crisis personal, we blame ourselves, even when we are blameless, or when there is no blame. (It's my fault I was laid off. I am not smart enough, creative enough, assertive enough.)

All of the "add-ons" affect how we feel and how we subsequently react. If we imagine things are going badly, we react that way. If we imagine things are going great, we react in kind. A more mature response is to get as close to the truth as possible before choosing what to feel and how to act.

Problem Analysis

The following process can help us get as close as possible to reality and an optimal choice.

Minimax

First, discover the minimum and maximum boundaries of the situation. Ask:

■ What is the worst that can happen? (The minimum.)

■ What is the best that can happen? (The maximum.)

■ What is realistic?

On the Pole, for example, the worst that can happen is that you might fall—about six inches. Or you might not get as high as you wish in front of your team. The best that can happen is that you might get all the way to the top, stand up, and pose for pictures taken by the admiring crowd. The most realistic outcome is that you will struggle a little, shake a bit, but you will go farther up the Pole than you thought you could, with your team's support.

Once you've put these kinds of boundaries around a problem, it loses some of its power and becomes more manageable. Minimax puts a floor on worst-case thinking so that you can focus on getting closer to the truth and solving the problem.

Getting to the Truth

What is the most accurate assessment of the situation? Here are some questions to ask:

■ What are the objective (observable, agreed upon) facts?

■ What are the rumors (statements based on opinion or theory, not grounded in observable facts)?

■ What am I making up?

■ What am I basing on past situations that may or may not be relevant?

■ Have I sought and listened to all points of view?

■ Am I listening to my intuition?

Only after we've looked objectively at the situation and understood it to the best of our abilities can we make a conscious choice.

Choose

Choosing is always the difficult part because it means taking action, making a commitment. The best choices are based on objective information and what is truly in our best interests.

Here are some things to think about:

■ Will my choice help me reach my goals?

■ Will it help me feel the way I want to feel?

- Will it help protect my life and health and that of my family?

- Will it help me avoid unwanted conflicts with others?

- Will it help me come closer to objective reality?

   With all that information, and as much objectivity as we can muster, we then make choices. Remember, Playing Not to Lose often involves making important choices unconsciously and irrationally, out of the desire to be comfortable. Playing to Win is about making important choices consciously, out of the desire to grow as a human being.

Financial Tools

> "People who run companies know that there are really only two critical factors in business. One is to make money and the other is to generate cash. As long as you do those two things your company will be okay, even if you make mistakes along the way, as you inevitably will. The only way to be secure is to make money and to generate cash. Everything else is a means to that end."
> — Jack Stack in *The Great Game of Business*

Vital Signs

The basics of financial vital signs apply to General Motors, the local hardware store, and you and me as individuals. These are the income statement, the balance sheet, and cash flow. Each can be summarized on the back of a napkin, or take up volumes of books, depending on the size and complexity of the organization. (More companies should use napkins instead of one-hundred-page computer printouts. But the M.B.A.'s and C.P.A.'s [the "A's" people] believe that complexity is somehow a virtue, so the trend is toward more paper and hard disk space, instead of less.)

Vital Sign No. 1. The Income Statement: How Much Did You Make and How Much Did It Cost?

Income: *The monetary payment received for goods or services, or from other sources, such as rents or investments, revenue receipts.*

The income statement, which can be published annually, quarterly, or even monthly, is a snapshot of an organization's or an individual's profitability over a period of time. The income statement is always historical information, a "rerun" of past financial events. In its most simple sense, the income statement reflects how much was taken in (income or sales) versus how much was spent (expenses).

Sales − Expenses = Income

As we have all no doubt learned, "income" doesn't always end up as a positive number. Expenses can sometimes (painfully) be greater than sales, which means that the income is negative, otherwise known as a loss.

Sales. "Sales" is usually listed first on an income statement. Again, depending on how many products or services a company sells and delivers, the sales entry can be one line or many pages.

The important thing to look at here is trends. What has happened to sales for the last few quarters? For the past few years? How has their share of the market changed over that period of time? These trends might be a result of price changes, new products, competition, or any number of other things. But by understanding where sales are and have been, you can start to see how you and your organization can positively impact where they might go.

Expenses. "Expenses" is the term that refers to all the funds that flow out of the organization's or the individual's bank account. Every check written by the company or the individual comes under one of the categories of expenses.

The important expense categories are cost of goods, sales, general and administrative expenses (SG&A), taxes and interest expense. By examining these numbers, you can see how much an organization or individual is spending in order to achieve a particular level of sales. The result indicates their level of profit or loss. Under those categories are expenses like research and development, rent, executive and administrative salaries.

The Corporate Levers. Driving business results, in essence, means helping customers *increase* sales or *decrease* expenses. The result of either is an increase in profitability on the infamous bottom line. If you cannot impact profitability or if you simply cannot explain or demonstrate how and where you can impact the two key levers of increasing sale or decreasing expenses, you are going to have a difficult time creating significant partnerships.

Vital Sign No. 2. The Balance Sheet: What Do You Own and What Do You Owe?

On one hand, you own your car and have paid down a large part of the mortgage on your house. On the other hand, you owe a lot on your credit cards, there is still a lot of mortgage to pay off, and, oh, yeah, there's that home equity loan you took out to build the new addition. . . .

Whether it's your personal finances or those of a large corporation, the balance sheet reflects basically the same premise: the balance between assets and liabilities. The balance sheet reflects the stability of a company or an individual at a specific time. It is another important financial vital sign that can be interpreted and used to find partnering opportunities.

The simple way to think about the balance sheet is to understand its three basic components and how they relate to each other. The components are:

Assets. Assets are resources available to the firm or the individual that have value now or will have value in the future. This can include current assets (such as cash, liquid cash investments, accounts receivable, and inventory), fixed assets (such as buildings, furniture, and equipment), intangible assets (such as patents, copyrights, goodwill, and trademarks), and long-term investments (over one year).

Add all those assets together—usually the right side of the ledger—and you obtain the asset bottom line: total assets, the number that represents the monetary value of what is owned.

Liabilities. Of course, for everything that your customers giveth, someone is standing in line to taketh away: liability. Liabilities are obligations to pay creditors or deliver services in the future.

There are two major categories of liabilities. The first is current liabilities (obligations that must be paid within one year), which include such items as accounts payable, accrued liabilities (like taxes, salaries, commissions, etc.), and short-term notes payable. The second category is long-term liabilities, things like money borrowed for more than one year.

In addition to assets and liabilities, the balance sheet also shows things like owners' equity (common stock, contributed capital, and retained earnings) and net worth (or book value). Taken altogether, what comes into focus is a snapshot of the health of a company. Once you become "fluent" in balance sheets for your customers, you begin to spot trends, problems (for example, very high accounts receivable balances compared to industry averages), and opportunities.

The Lifeblood. But income statements and balance sheets don't necessarily give you a sense of the other critical, "life-giving" asset of a business (or definitely a household): CASH!

Vital Sign No. 3. The Cash Flow Statement: How Much Came in and How Much Was Sucked Out?

A company can be profitable, have a "model" balance sheet, and still run out of cash and thus out of business. Why?

Timing is everything, especially when it comes to cash. More important than end-of-the-year profitability is a business's ability to generate "positive cash flow" every month. At the most basic level, that means the amount of cash coming into the company from all sources is equal to or hopefully greater than the amount of cash going out.

Stockholders, boards of directors, and Wall Street are interested in profits at the end of the year. But the people that operate a company fixate on cash flow, the monthly "nut." As CEO of a business for the last thirty years, what has kept me up pacing the halls late at night isn't profitability—it is whether or not next month, or next quarter, we will have cash on hand to pay the bills. It can become very simple, very black and white.

A quick aside. If you can't seem to get your customers to focus on long-term strategic thinking, that might be a symptom that they routinely are obsessed by whether or not they are going to run out of money. Having been in that situation a number of times in my career, I can assure you that everything else pales in importance. Running out of money in the short term has an amazing ability to focus the mind. Strategic planning, new equipment, training, business plans—all of that stuff goes out the window and the cry becomes: Find cash!!

To anyone running a household, cash flow should be familiar. The same principles apply. You can have a great "net worth," but if the bills—the mortgage, the utilities, car payments, school payments, and credit card payments— exceed what you take in each month, or even if you cover your expenses but you aren't saving any money (the personal equivalent of profitability), your long-term prognosis is not healthy: a lifestyle change is probably required.

And, of course, the business landscape is littered with companies that are having to change their lifestyle for much the same reasons—cash going out exceeds cash coming in. So what do they do? Back to those same two levers. They can choose to reduce monthly expenses, which eventually frees up cash. Or they can attempt to increase cash flow into the company, either by increasing sales by decreasing prices (which increases cash flow at the expense of profitability), selling off assets, or borrowing money (which can lead to longer-term cash flow problems—all that debt adds up to more cash out monthly and so on and so on).

Like every part of the business equation, managing cash

flow is a balancing art. There needs to be enough cash on hand, but not at the expense of failing to invest in people, new technologies, and the like. But let's face it: today the scramble is for cash and that is keeping a lot of your customers awake at night.

Compared with What?

As the old saying goes, "There are three kinds of lies: lies, damned lies and statistics." The problem with numbers, especially those expressed in our three business vital signs, is that they are meaningless and easily distorted without the right context. If a nurse only tells a doctor, "The patient has a pulse of one hundred," that is not helpful information. In the same manner, a number off the bottom of the income statement tells you nothing in and of itself. The total revenue of any company as a single number is useless, not only to a financial analyst but to a consultant trying to understand where the leverage points might be for developing a financially relevant partnering relationship.

The ability to diagnose, to make sense out of the raw numbers, comes with seeing them in context—in relationship to other factors and other numbers. In the world of finance, we look at trends and ratios.

Trends

When a sick or hurt patient is brought in to an emergency room, a good medical team isn't just interested in the patient's vital signs at that moment. They expect the ambulance paramedics to be able to tell them what the trend of the vital signs has been. They want to know the history of the patient—what happened and when did it happen? With that kind of information, a good medical team can begin to put together the whole picture.

It's the same with diagnosing a business, whether it's "sick" or vibrantly healthy. What is important is the trend, the financial history. Pick any item on an income statement and compare it with the same number for the last three to five years. How has it changed? Has it gone up or down? Then compare another item and its trends in the same time frame. If profits have gone up, is it because sales have gone up? Have profits gone up the same percentage that sales have gone up? Have profits grown at a greater or lesser rate than sales?

For example, if the trend in profitability is lagging behind that of sales growth, that may indicate that costs are out of control, or perhaps margins on sales are under pressure. What does it mean when margins are under pressure? Are salespeople having to give on prices? Is there more competition? You can go on and on.

When you look at trends, you can begin to see the entire picture and hone in on crucial issues. Once you understand the financial trends of a company, you begin to see the world through the eyes of their senior management. You begin to understand what questions they walk around with all day (How do we cut costs? How can we turn our inventory faster?) and what solutions may be valued by them.

Ratios

Comparing numbers with other numbers is called a ratio. Ratios of financial numbers are another diagnostic tool that is used with financial statements to understand a business better. Again, it is like being part of the medical team trying to diagnose a sick patient. Every medical team has crammed into their brains sets of ratios. This is based on the statistical analysis of millions of patients and by that doctor's personal experience. For example, there is a set range of the ratio between white blood cells to red blood cells. A team sees a hundred or so patients a week, and they see the same ratio. Then a patient comes in, the ratio is outside of the "norm," and red flags go up. The medical team dives in to find out why that is so, what is causing the difference.

In the same way, you can use ratios to examine the financial status of a customer to see where it falls in comparison to norms. Some useful diagnostic tools that use ratios are common size analysis (a ratio that allows you to compare different-size companies) and ratio analysis (comparing company to company, company to their industry, and company to other industries).

At the end of this resource section are listed several other common ratio tools that can be used to diagnose and to compare key indicators to other companies and other industries. Some will be appropriate for your business and your customer, and some won't. Use the ones that you think apply and run ratios on a couple of your customers. Compare the results. Find the differences, and try to locate the causes of those differences.

The fun part of business is using these kinds of tools to explore, to be a detective, and to get at what is really going on inside your customer's organization. Then you can begin to imagine and create highly relevant and easy-to-sell solutions—solutions that can lead to high-gain partnering relationships.

Important Safety Tip

Unless you are really inside an organization, it is very difficult to determine without a shadow of a doubt what the causes are for the numbers, trends, and ratios listed in the income statement, balance sheet, and cash flow statement. As a result, the reason you need to become fluent in reading and understanding financial reports is to *generate questions*. The answers won't often be in the numbers—at least not all of them. The best use of these reports is to raise issues and areas of concern that you can discuss with your customers.

When you're calling high, on CEOs and CFOs, the idea is not to walk in and say, "Hey, I read your income statement—boy, are you guys in trouble! It's a good thing I came in today, huh?"

Rather, the smart partnering salesperson will use the financials as a "jumping off point," a place to start asking questions and gathering important information that can then—and only then—help you discover and formulate high-value solutions.

Parlez-vous français?

When I was a lot younger, and more confident of my linguistic abilities, I spent some time in Paris. Having just completed a cram course in French, I was pretty sure that I could *"parlez-vous"* with the best of them. Excited about exploring Paris, I got on the subway early one morning during rush hour. I was instantly bombarded by more and faster French than I had ever heard or dreamed possible. I had no idea where I was or where I should get off. I panicked and, using the only French I could remember, I asked the woman standing next to me if she spoke English. She looked at me with the disdain that only the French seem to have truly mastered. It at once showed shock that I would even attempt to speak to her in her native language, and contempt for my Minnesota accent.

These last few pages have been a thumbnail sketch of some of the key words and phrases in the language of finance. It's the equivalent of having just enough understanding to get you onto a subway (just enough to really get you into trouble). There is a whole world of financial speakers out there, from beginners to generalists to people who specialize in the minutiae—like tax implications. Adding to that is the special language—the regional dialects, if you will, of your customers and your industry.

Further, we've no doubt left out whole encyclopedias' worth of critical financial information. For example, currency exchange rates between nations could be argued to be fundamental to understanding the business environment of many companies—and all companies within the next ten years.

The point is that there is a lot going on financially in companies that is beyond the scope of this book. The larger the company, the more that is so. The only way to get your arms around your customers, and their reality, is to study, to ask questions, to tune in to the financial world and marketplace that you and your customers exist in. Read the *Wall Street Journal*. Subscribe to a clipping service. Study the annual reports. Get a mentor if you need one. But learn the language.

Depending on your customers and their needs, you only might be required to say, "Good morning and how are you?" in financial speak. Or you might have to be one of the specialists. In any case, the language of finance is the language of business, it is the driver now and into the fore-seeable future of most high-level business relationships.

Making the Business Case

When you are fluent in the language, you can speak to your customers, especially senior management, in ways they will listen to and respect. You are no longer talking about product, you are talking about their bottom line—the issues that are nearest and dearest to them. When they believe that you

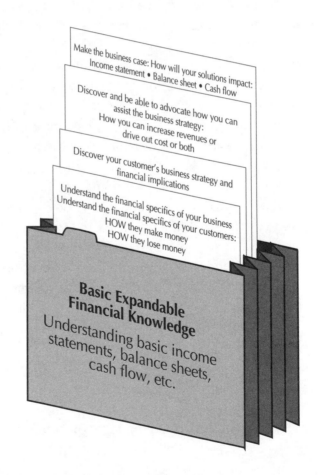

Make the business case: How will your solutions impact:
Income statement • Balance sheet • Cash flow

Discover and be able to advocate how you can assist the business strategy:
How you can increase revenues or drive out cost or both

Discover your customer's business strategy and financial implications

Understand the financial specifics of your business
Understand the financial specifics of your customers:
HOW they make money
HOW they lose money

Basic Expandable Financial Knowledge
Understanding basic income statements, balance sheets, cash flow, etc.

understand their world, they'll listen. When you understand why your customer's company "comes to work"—how they make money, how they lose money, and what their financial world looks like—you are then primed to help them where it counts most. You can start to see the financial opportunities and where you can help and leverage. You can make the business case. That is true competitive advantage and that is what we are all trying to create.

Formula and Ratios

The formula to use to get the percentage of change from year to year is:

$$\frac{\text{Current year's amount} - \text{Last year's amount}}{\text{Last year's amount}}$$

Accounts Receivable Turnover. Accounts receivable turnover is a measure of how well a company is collecting its receivable.

Accounts receivable turnover = Sales/Accounts receivable

Return on Equity. Return on equity is an investment return ratio measured as net income divided by equity.

Return on equity = Net income/Equity

Current Ratio. Current ratio measures a company's liquidity (the ability to cover short-term liabilities using the company's liquid assets).

Current ratio = Current assets/Current liabilities

Financial Leverage. Financial leverage is the use of debt to increase the expected return on equity.

Financial leverage = Assets/Total equity

Inventory Turnover. Inventory turnover is the number of times the average inventory has been sold during a period.

Inventory turnover = Sales/Inventory

Asset Turnover. Asset turnover measures how effectively assets are generating sales and shows that each dollar invested in assets yields "X" dollars in sales.

Asset turnover = Sales/Assets

References

Calvin, William, *The River That Flows Upstream*. San Francisco: Sierra Club Books, 1986.

Frangos, Stephen J., *Team Zebra*. Essex Junction, VT: Oliver Wight Publications, 1993.

Levitt, Theodore, *The Marketing Imagination*. New York: The Free Press, 1983.

Stack, Jack, *The Great Game of Business*. New York: Doubleday/ Currency, 1992.

Toffler, Alvin, *Future Shock*. New York: Random House, 1970.

————*The Third Wave*. New York: Random House, 1980.

Watzlawick, Paul, et al., *Change: Principles of Problem Formation and Problem Resolution*. New York: W. W. Norton, 1974.

Wilson, Larry, and Wilson, Hersch, *Changing the Game: The New Way to Sell*. New York: Simon and Schuster, 1987.

Index

If you would like more information about Pecos River
Learning Centers Inc. or about Partnering: Creating
Customers for Life, please call:

Pecos River Learning Centers Inc.
Sales and Market Support Center
7600 Executive Drive
Eden Prairie, Minnesota 55344
(612) 975-2100
Fax (612) 975-2199